Understanding Storytelling Among African American Children: A Journey From Africa to America

Understanding Storytelling Among African American Children: A Journey From Africa to America

Tempii B. Champion
University of South Florida

LAWRENCE ERLBAUM ASSOCIATES, PUBLISHERS

2003   Mahwah, New Jersey   London

Senior Acquisitions Editor	Naomi Silverman
Editorial Assistant:	Erica Kica
Cover Photograph:	Arthur M. Guilford
Cover Design:	Kathryn Houghtaling Lacey
Textbook Production Manager:	Paul Smolenski
Text and Cover Printer:	Sheridan Books

The camera ready copy for the text of this book was provided by the author.

Lawrence Erlbaum Associates, Inc., Publishers
10 Industrial Avenue
Mahwah, New Jersey 07430

Library of Congress Cataloging-in-Publication Data

Champion, Tempii.
Understanding storytelling among African American children : a journey from Africa to
  America / Tempii Champion.
    p.   cm.
  Includes bibliographical references and indexes.
  ISBN 0-8058-3407-9 (alk. paper)
1. African American children–Language. 2. English language–United States–Foreign ele-
  ments–African.   3. English language–United States–Discourse analysis.   4. English
  Language–United States–Rhetoric. 5. African languages–Influence on English. 6. Sto-
  rytelling–United States. 7. Storytelling–Africa.   8. Narration (Rhetoric)   I. Title.
PE3102.N42 C47 2002
808.5'43'08996073–dc21   2002069203

Printed in the United States of America
10 9 8 7 6 5 4 3 2 1

Dedication

Dr. Lynda Ruth Campbell
April 1958 – March 2001

Ancestors are remembered as long as there is someone to call their names. This book is dedicated to Dr. Lynda Ruth Campbell, who returned home to be with her parents on March 15, 2001. Lynda's love and commitment to providing innovative language research among African American children and collegial support for young scholars have impacted many lives, and the fruits of her labor are in her writings and those she touched. Lynda's encouragement, laughter and comforting presence, before and after her death, have made this book possible.

Contents

Preface

This book reports research on narrative production among African American children for the purpose of extending previous research and discussion of narrative structure. Some researchers studying narrative production among African American children have focused on the influence of culture on the narrative structures employed. Some researchers (e.g., Michaels, 1981; Heath, 1983; Gee, 1985) have suggested that narrative structure is strongly influenced by home culture. Other researchers (Hyon & Sulzby, 1994; Hicks & Kanvesky, 1992) have suggested that the narrative structures produced are not necessarily affiliated with the home culture of the child. They find that African American children, like children in general, often produce narrative structures typically found in school settings.

The research in this book extends previous research on narrative structures produced by African American children by suggesting that African American children do not produce one structure of narratives exclusively, as previously reported. My research suggests that African American children produce a repertoire of narrative structures. Some of the narrative structures found appear to have links to African and African American narrative structures, whereas other structures are similar to European American narrative structures.

Overview of the book

Chapter 1 provides an introduction to the book. Areas covered in this chapter include the history of storytelling within the African American community, transformation from African to African American, African American English language studies, narrative analysis and purpose of the book. The book is divided into three parts.

Part 1, "Approaches to Understanding Narrative Structures Among African American Children"(chapters 2 -4 of the book) provides a framework for understanding narrative structures among African American children. Chapter 2 presents an overview of research narrative structures among African Americans and West Africans. The African and African American cultures have a rich oral tradition within oral storytelling strategies. In chapter 3, I present the research design and procedures of the study presented in this book, and address how the study builds on and extends the research on narrative production among African American children. Because my perspective values the culture and social processes in which children develop, a mixed research designed was employed.

Part II, Toward a Repertoire of Narrative Structures Among African American Children (chapters 5 -7), provides evidence that African American children produce a repertoire narrative structures that are complex in nature. The narratives that were produced by the children in this study suggest speculatively that there may be links to African American culture and possibly West African culture. The first two chapters of Part II examine narratives using two traditional analyses. In chapter 4, results are reported using evaluative analysis. The participants produced the classic structure most frequently. In chapter 5, the episodic analysis yielded similar results with complex structures produced the most. Chapter 6 presents results using thematic and some aspects of West African narrative strategies to analyze narratives. These narratives have been coded as "moral centered." In chapter 7, narratives are coded as "performative" using thematic and sociolinguistic analyses.

Part III, Research to Practice, connects the research findings to implications of educating African American students. This area is comprised of one chapter (chapter 8) which examines educational implications under four broad categories: home-school mismatch; teacher expectations; culturally relevant pedagogy and narrative instruction. Direction for the future research is also presented. This book is appropriate for areas of education, African American studies, Communication, Psychology and Communication Sciences and Disorders. The book provides detailed analyses of narratives using both psychological text analysis and qualitative analysis.

Acknowledgments

Helpful comments on drafts of this book were received from the following individuals: Allyssa McCabe, Joy James, Ruth Bahr, Arthur Guilford, Jane Scheurle, Lynda Campbell, David Bloome, and Christine Probes. In addition, I would like to thank the reviewers commissioned by Lawrence Erlbaum Associates: Sonja L. Lanchart, University of Georgia, Denise Troutman, Michigan Sate University and two anonymous reviewers, your comments were very helpful in my revision of the book. I would also like to thank Susan Friedman and Laurel Jaffer for their editorial work on this book. Thanks to Naomi Silverman for her valuable feedback and encouragement throughout the process of writing this book. The writing of this manuscript was supported by funds from the National Institute on Deafness and other Communication Disorders (KO1 DC00160 04).

**Understanding Storytelling Among
African American Children:
A Journey From Africa to America**

1
Tell Me Somethin' Good:
Storytelling From Africa to America

There were two mischievous boys who decided they would fool the old wise man of the community. "He thinks he's so smart," they thought. "We will trick him." One day, they decided they would show him a bird in their hands and ask him, "This bird in my hands, is it dead or alive?" They agreed that if the old man replied "It is dead" they would let the bird go free, but if he answered "It is alive," they would crush the bird. So they went to the old man and posed the question: "Old man . . . Old man, this bird that we hold in our hands, is it dead or alive?" Without a pause the old man responded, "It's in your hands."

Fannie Lou Hamer, a grass roots civil rights activist, told this story more than 40 years ago to motivate civil rights workers to fight for social justice for African Americans. This same story motivates the research and writing of this book on the importance of storytelling in the lives of children, especially African American children, from the ages of 6 to 10 years old.

History of Storytelling Within the African American Community

Storytelling in the African American community traveled a long way from Africa to United States. In West Africa, storytelling was one of the cultural and social practices that Africans participated in during various aspects of their daily lives. The art of storytelling was used both to teach and to comfort members of the community. Storytelling helped to preserve history—of one's self, one's family, and one's ethnic group. Among the ancient stories retold today are those about creation and the tales of gods. As an example, we have an excerpt from "How Sky and Earth Became One: A Yoruba Creation Story," told by Ralph Cheo Thurman (cited in Williams, 1997), which illustrates a community's belief of a spiritual beginning:

On creation eve, Obatala and Orunmilla sat in the perfect light of the sky as they looked down at the earth, into the mysterious and dark domain of the sea goddess, Olokun. Obatala sat on a throne made from a huge elephant tusk; Orunmilla's throne, made from a kola nut, was trimmed with sixteen cowrie shells. As they watched and waited and pondered the mystery of the sea, Obatala carved human figurines from the white wood of a tree found only in their father's garden.

Obatala dropped the figurines. One by one they fell through marshmallow clouds and splashed mightily into Olokun's great sea. Olokun accepted Obatala's gifts with a splash of salty sea on Obatala's feet. When his feet dried, Obatala scraped off the salt and shared it with the other Orisas in Orun, the dwelling place of the divine beings.

Obatala was a great artist, so his father Olorun often sent him to planets to mold and shape humans in the images of the different Orisas. Once created, Olorun would breathe life into the humans, and the Orisas would claim them as their children. The Orisas taught their human children the wisdom and power of earth and the sky. And when the humans finished their earthly tasks, the Orisas showed them the way back home.Orunmilla," said Obatala. "Look at the endless water and darkness on the earth. Even you have said that Earth is a sore eye to the universe. Of all the millions of planets I've created, only Earth remains empty, lifeless."

"Do you think the Earth is ready for life?" asked Orunmilla. Obatala shrugged. "Only Olorun can answer that question." Obatala and Orunmilla assumed a meditative posture and contemplated the plight of earth for eternities. They waited for a message from Olorun.

Obatala uttered a secret prayer to Olorun, and at that moment Orunmilla opened his left hand, then the right one. Obatala smiled at the sign. Olorun had granted him his desire to make Earth a livable planet. (pp. 57-58)

This creation story enabled the Yoruba community in western Nigeria to make sense of their world. The narrative begins with two spiritual beings, Obatala and Orunmilla, contemplating the future of Earth. In this myth, human beings were made by Obatala, the great artist, and Olorun breathed life into them. Olorun appears to be the Supreme Being because he granted the prayers of Obatala. This creation myth teaches believers in the Yoruba cosmetology that god (Olorun) grants wishes by prayers. In addition, they are taught that the creation of a livable earth was a combined effort by Obatala, Orunmilla and Olorun.

The cultural and social practices of West Africa traveled with Africans as they crossed the waters to the United States. Despite the horrors of slavery, Africans (now African Americans) still told stories to comfort, teach, and record history in their new home. The stories now incorporated a different language—a language that had been used to oppress and enslave the African. Africans took the language forced on them and interwove patterns of their native languages with this new language. These storytelling traditions continued from slavery through Jim Crowism, to the Civil Rights movement, and on to present= day America.

Brewer (1972) has commented that these home stories have made their way to America or wherever the African lives. Within the transported Africans' new contexts they adapted their former home stories to fit the needs of their present home, thereby creating the Anansi and the trickster stories. These folktales usually embedded a moral message in them. Stories were never told for the sake of entertainment, but were used instead to enable the hearer to grow morally and spiritually.

Levine's (1977) study of Black culture describes African American storytelling as both performance and moralizing agents. Levine observed, "The oral inventiveness of good storytellers, who appear to have been relatively common in black culture, was a source of delight and stimulation to their audiences. Their narratives were interlarded with chants, mimicry, rhymes and songs" (p. 88). Levine also stated that narrative performances could include paralinguistic features along with body movements. Smitherman (1977) concurs with Levine, stating that storytellers become the words they convey; that is, they use both voice and body movement as tools to convey their stories.

According to Levine (1977), narratives from the emancipation period up to the 1960s were often infused with a direct moral message. Moral messages, whether implicit or explicit, were quite common in Africa. Smitherman (1977) explained that "narrative forms have as their overriding theme coping ability, strength, endurance, trickeration capacity and power of black people" (p. 156).

"A Remedy for Racism" by Dick Gregory (cited in Williams, 1997) displays the coping ability that Smitherman (1977) discusses:

> Last time I was down South I walked into this restaurant, and this white waitress came up to me and said: "We don't serve colored people here." I said: "That's all right, I don't eat colored people. Bring me a whole fried chicken." About that time these three cousins come in, you know the ones I mean, Klu, Kluck, and Klan, and they say: "Boy, we're givin' you fair warnin." Anything you do to that chicken, we're gonna do to you." About then the waitress brought me my chicken. "Remember, boy, anything you do that chicken, we're gonna do to you." So I put down my knife and fork, and I picked up that chicken, and I kissed it. (p. 213)

In this narrative, Gregory uses humor to cope with racism. Okpewho (1992) suggested that humor was also used within West African storytelling as a technique to impart a moral lesson. Some researchers (Levine, 1977; Smitherman, 1977) suggest that storytelling within the African American community has a continuing link to African culture. J. Mason Brewer (1972) observed this continuity between Africa and African American culture:

> The folk literature of the American Negro has a rich inheritance from its African background. . . . They brought with them no material possessions to aid in preserving the arts and customs of their homeland. Yet though empty handed perforce they carried in their minds and hearts a treasure of complex musical forms, dramatic speech, and imaginative stories, which they perpetuated through the vital art of self expression. Wherever the slaves were ultimately placed they established an enclave of African culture that flourished in spite of environmental disadvantages . . . (p. 3)

The study of Africanisms within American culture has been examined by Herkovitz (1941), Puckett (1936), Woodson (1933), DuBois (1933), Turner (1949), Whitten and Szwed (1970), and Levine (1977). Collectively, these researchers provide evidence that African Americans have a past beyond the United States. The preservation of African characteristics was found in African American religion, music, dance, language, and oratory skills.

African to African American

African Americans have been in the United States more than 400 years. The majority of African American ancestors were brought to the United States on slave ships. Africans were captured from Guinea-Bissau, Guinea, Sierra Leone, the Ivory Coast, Ghana, the bight of Biafra, and West Central Africa, the bight of Biafra and West Central Africa being the areas from which most African Americans descended.

The transformation from African to African American included four stages of acculturation: the initial capture, the barracoon stage, the transatlantic voyage, and the seasoning stage (Gomez, 1999). The initial capture of the Africans was the first stage of this transformation—from African to African American.

The barracoon stage began when Africans were transferred along the coast to different ports of departure to await embarkation. The barracoons were structures that housed Africans. Structures ranged in comfort from pens to castles. On my travels to Africa, I visited a barracoon in Dakar, Senegal, on the island of Goree. The structure resembles a two-level castle. The lower level is where the Africans were housed. There were three separate rooms, one each for women, men, and children. The upper level, which was more spacious, was for the European traders. On the door leading outside for embarkation I read the following inscription: "Through this door for a voyage without return, they would go with their eyes fixed on the infinity of their suffering."

The next stage was the middle passage or the transatlantic voyage. In St. Louis, the Black Wax Museum houses a replica of an actual slave ship that allows visitors to see how the Africans were shackled and tightly packed on the ships, able only to lie on their backs and sides, often remaining in these positions for long periods of time.

The last stage in the transformation process was seasoning. This period could last from 1 to 3 years. During this time the African adjusted to different clothes, foods, and a new language. Gomez (1999) has stated that maintaining their native language as well as acquiring a new language was a powerful tool in the transformation process. He suggested that during the seasoning stage Africans continued using their native language, and that the use of English was an individual choice. Furthermore, Africans may have learned English, but added Africanisms to it, thereby creating a unique style of English. The dialect that has developed from this transformation from being African to becoming African American is called African American English (AAE).

African American English Language Studies

In the last 30 years, linguists such as Labov (1969), Wolfram (1971), Dalby (1972), Dillard (1972), Vaughn-Cooke (1976), and Smitherman (1977), among others, have examined the linguistic features of African American English (formerly called "Black English"). The claim that AAE was an inferior dialect was strongly denounced, and these experts demonstrated that AAE is a systematic, rule-governed dialect equal to any other dialect of English, including Standard English.

During the same period, studies were conducted with AAE child speakers, specifically focusing on grammatical and lexical aspects of language acquisition. Research by Steffensen (1974), Kovak (1980), Stokes (1976), Reveron (1978), Cole (1980), H. Seymour and C. Seymour (1981), and H. Seymour and Ralabate (1985) focused on structural syntax, phonology, and lexical components of AAE. Early language studies rarely considered discourse development, most notably narrative production.

In addition, these studies tended to analyze only single sentences extracted from language samples. The range of strategies that children use to reveal their communicative competence, however, cannot be explicated from the study of single sentences explored in isolation. Linguistic features do not operate in isolation, but from social and meaningful contexts; the study of child language acquisition may be more revealing when social context is also considered.

Narrative Analysis

Narrative analysis can reveal children's strategies for organizing, comprehending, and producing language (Liles, 1987, 1993). Because narrative production reveals a broader range of acquisition properties, narratives have been used with increasing frequency during speech and language evaluations (Scott, 1988; Liles, 1985; Westby, 1984). Narratives also reveal how different cultural groups organize and make sense of their world (Bruner, 1985). As Taylor (1988) contends, "Narrative competence is developmental . . . the socialization which undergirds this development varies across cultures" (p. 19).

Educators are using narrative production analysis more frequently among children in the classroom. In addition, speech language pathologists use narrative analysis within language evaluations with children and adults. Results of language evaluations have been used for educational planning and language intervention. It is important to have various analytical tools that take into account children's cultural backgrounds and discourse styles for an informed evaluation of narratives.

Traditional approaches to narrative analysis may have penalized children from culturally or linguistically diverse populations. Currently, the majority of research on narrative analysis focuses on children from European American backgrounds. Because narrative production may be shaped by children's socialization processes, it is not clear that current narrative analysis procedures are appropriate for children from cultural and linguistic backgrounds that are not European Americans. The lack of appropriate models and procedures for understanding the narratives produced by children from non- European American cultural and linguistic groups often results in an over-identification of language learning problems, which can lead to inappropriate educational placements and services.

Purpose

This book reports research on narrative production among African American children for the purpose of extending previous research and discussion of narrative structure. Some researchers studying narrative production among African American children have focused on the influence of culture on the narrative structures employed. One group of researchers (Michaels, 1981; Heath, 1983; Gee, 1985) has suggested that narrative structure is strongly influenced by home culture. This group of researchers indicated that some African American children produce narratives that are a series of associated segments linked together implicitly to a topic. This type of narrative is termed "topic associating" by Michaels (1981). Michaels reported that "topic associating" narratives appear to have connections to African American culture. In her research, African American children produced these narratives the majority of the time.

Other researchers (Hyon & Sulzby, 1994; Hicks & Kanevsky, 1992) have suggested that the narrative structures produced are not necessarily affiliated with the home culture of the child. They find that African American children, like children in general, often produce narrative structures typically found in school settings. These narratives are tightly structured discourses on a single topic and are linked together explicitly. This type of narrative is termed "topic centered" by Michaels (1981), who found it used exclusively by European American children. Results of the various studies raise questions regarding the type of narrative structures African American children produce as well as suggesting broader questions about the range and types of narrative structures.

One way to interpret the extant research on the narrative structures produced by African American children is to consider that African American children employ multiple structures for telling stories and are influenced by a broad range of factors, including cultural backgrounds, specific interpersonal settings, and elicitation methods, among other factors. The findings in this book extend previous research on narrative structures produced by African American children by suggesting that African American children do not produce one structure of narratives exclusively, as previously reported. My research suggests that African American children produce a repertoire of narrative structures. Some of the narrative structures appear to have links to African and African American narrative structures, wheareas others are similar to European American narrative structures. Given that African American children have been socialized by both African American and European American cultural values these the findings are not surprising.

PART 1
Approaches to Understanding Narrative Structures Among African American Children

The goal of this book is to extend the research on narrative production among African American children by emphasizing the repertoire of narrative structures produced depending upon the prompts used to elicit narratives. Part I provides a framework for understanding narrative structures among African American children. Chapter 2 presents an overview of research narrative structures among African Americans and West Africans. The perspective presented here is that narrative production by African American children is grounded in the cultural and social processes in the African American community. The African American culture has a rich oral tradition with roots in West African oral storytelling. African American children are socialized toward this oral tradition from a young age in different community contexts such as the church and the playground. When children enter school, they encounter a socialization process that may or may not be similar to their home culture. Some African American children, however, have mastered the narrative structures of the school culture. Thus, some African American children produce a range of narrative structures with some structures representing the culture of their community and others representing the culture of school.

Chapter 3 outlines the research design and procedures of the study presented in this book and addresses how the study builds on and extends the research on narrative production among African American children. Because my perspective values the culture and social processes of children's experiences, a mixed research designed was employed. The analysis presented in this chapter examines narratives from school (mainstream) and home (culture) perspectives.

2
Research on Narrative Structures Among African Americans and West Africans

Research on Narrative Production Among African American Children

Researchers have described African American children's narrative structures as complex as those of middle=class European American children, although the structures differ (Michaels, 1981; Michaels & Foster, 1985; Michaels & Collins, 1984).

Michaels and Cook-Gumperz (1979) conducted a study focusing on "show and tell" narratives (later termed sharing time narratives) with children in a first=grade classroom in Berkeley, California. When differentiating between European American and African American, Michaels (1981) used the terms topic centered and topic associating, respectively. Topic centered narratives were defined as "tightly organized centering on a single clearly identifiable topic and thematic development . . . characteristically achieved through a linear progression of information " (p. 428), whereas topic associating narratives were a "discourse consisting of a series of implicitly associated personal anecdotes" (p. 429).

Researchers looked not only at the children but also at the teacher's role in sharing. Michaels and Cook-Gumperz (1979) found that the teacher's comments collaborated and helped with narrative discourse if both the teacher and the child agreed in their expectations of what comprised a good narrative. Within the sharing time in the classroom, Michaels and Cook-Gumperz reported that the teacher had difficulty scaffolding the narratives of the African American children but not with the European American. Also, the teacher interrupted and restated directions to the African American children more often than for the European American.

Table 2.1 shows a summary of Michael's findings as described by Gee (1985).

TABLE 2.1

TOPIC CENTERED VERSUS TOPIC ASSOCIATING

Topic Centered	Topic Associating
Tightly structured discourse on single topic or series of closely related topics.	A series of associated segments that may seem anecdotal in character, linked implicitly to particular topical event or theme, but with no explicit statement of an overall theme or point.
Lexically explicit referential, temporal, and spatial relationships. No major shifts in perspective, temporal orientation or thematic focus.	
High degree of thematic coherence and a clear thematic progression.	While these stories start with time, person, and place, temporal orientation, location, and focus often shift across segments—these shifts are marked by shifts in pitch contours and tempo often accompanied by a formulaic time marker.
Begin with temporal grounding a statement of focus, introducing key agents, and some indication of spatial grounding. Orientation is followed by elaboration on topic.	
The child marks syntactically complete, independent clauses with special time intonation (high rising tone with vowel elongation) that means "more to come" and demarcates the clause as an information unit.	Relationship between parts of the narrative have to be inferred by the listener.
	Temporal indicators (yesterday, last night, tomorrow) occur more than once.
Finishes with a punch line sort of resolution, signaled by a markedly lower pitch or falling tone stories tend to be short and concise.	The special sharing time intonation is used not to mark continuity, but to highlight discontinuity, marking the separation of narrative segments and shifts in temporal orientation, location or focus.
Stories tend to be short and concise.	The stories may give the impression to those who have no control over the style of having no beginning, no end-thus no point.
	Stories tend to be longer.

Michaels and Foster (1985) studied a first-second grade classroom where the children were in charge of "sharing time." There were "no teacher rules governing topic, style, or amount of time that each person can talk" (p. 145). The children in the classroom decided what was appropriate sharing.

Two styles of narratives emerged from the student-run sharing time: the "lecture demonstration" and the "performed narrative." European American children tended to use the lecture demonstration while African American children tended to use the performed narrative style. Michaels and Foster (1985) defined lecture demonstration as a narrative "about an object or event, a presentation of a factual information," and the performed narrative as a "personal narrative account, emphasizing interaction between two or more people" (p. 145).

The children appreciated both styles of narratives. The implicit notions about correctness previously present in Michaels and Cook-Gumperz (1979) and Michaels (1981) were absent. The most important aspect in a student-run sharing time is keeping audience interest. The authors concluded by emphasizing the importance of being allowed to "fully demonstrate the narrative and descriptive discourse skills they bring with them from home, and build upon this competence and sophistication in the classroom" (Michaels & Foster, 1985, p. 157). This study utilized an alternate analysis of language use within different cultures, in that it did not use a preferred model as a reference point (i.e., Standard English). Each culture was valued as important to children's development and competency in their use of discourse skills. Table 2.2 summarizes Michaels and Foster 's 1985 findings.

TABLE 2.2

Lecture Demonstration Versus Performed Narrative

Lecture Demonstration	Performed Narrative
• presentation of factual information	• narrative account emphasizing interaction between friends and/or relatives
• tends to be about an object	
• uses marked school register	• stylistic devices:
• enunciates clearly	- extra loudness
• solicits questions from audience	- gestures
• formal and instructional	- shifts to present tense dialogue

In the same light, Heath (1983) conducted an ethnographic study of three communities in the Piedmont area of Virginia. The communities consisted of (a) a working-class African American community, (b) a White and African American middle-class community, and (c) a working-class White community. Heath's study, like previous studies (Michaels & Cook-Gumperz, 1979; Michaels, 1981), observed children prior to their beginning school. In all communities, children were socialized differently to literacy.

The middle-class children were socialized toward school literacy from an early age. Children were read topic-centered stories that matched the discourse in a school setting. While the working-class European American children were also read to, their parents did not link the events in books to events in life. On the other hand, the African American working-class children interacted socially with adults and children on a continuous basis. During these interactions children were rewarded for verbal and nonverbal behavior. Heath's (1983) description of narrative skills development of the working-class African American children is summarized here:

Repetition stage. Children imitate intonation patterns during the repetition of utterances. An example from Heath's data includes Lem, age 14 months:

> Mother [talking to neighbor on porch while Lem plays with a truck
> on the porch nearby]: But they won't call back won't happen Lem:
> call back Neighbor: Sam's going over there Saturday, he'll pick up a
> form Lem: pick up on, pick up on [Lem here appears to have heard
> "form" as "on"] (p. 114)

Repetition with variation stage. Children incorporate conversation into talk as they play. An example of Lem (at 26 months) is again presented:

> Mother: She went to the doctor again Lem: went to de doctor,
> doctor, tractor, dis my tractor [in a singsong fashion] doctor on a
> tractor, went to de doctor (p. 114).

Participation stage. Children at this stage enter ongoing conversation. It is at this stage (between the ages of 2 and 4 years) that children produce monologue-like stories. Lem, at age 30 months, demonstrates this stage:

Way	You hear it?
Far Now	Far
It a churchbell	Now (p. 115)
Ringin'	

As far as narratives are concerned, once in school working-class European American and African American children encountered different notions of truth, style, and language appropriate to a story from those they had known at home. The working-class European American community allows only factual and concise stories, while the working-class African American community narratives were more creative than factual. These characteristics of narration in both communities contradicted what were classroom expectations, causing both groups of children to experience difficulty in the classroom. The research by Heath (1983) and Michaels (1981) broke new ground and afforded important insights about the influence of home culture on narrative production. Before these studies, the culture of African American children was not considered when describing narrative production. With the acknowledgement of cultural importance, new findings by Hyon & Sulzby (1994), Champion, Seymour and Camarata, (1995), Champion, Katz, Muldrow and Dial (1999); Hester (1996), Bloome, Champion, Katz, Morton and Muldrow (2001) have shown that African American children produce a range of narrative structures.

In their study of narrative production, Hyon & Sulzby (1994) found that African American children used topic centered narrative structures (typically associated with middle-class European American children) more frequently than topic associating narrative structures (typically associated with African American children). Similarly, using episodic analysis and evaluative analysis, Champion, Seymour, & Camarata (1995) found that the African American children they studied produced a range of complex and sophisticated narrative structures. In this study, the researchers questioned the limitations of episodic and evaluative analyses due to their linear structure.

In a series of articles and papers, Bloome, Champion and Katz (1997), and Champion, Katz, Muldrow & Dail (1999) examined the production of written and spoken narratives among three different groups of African American preschoolers over a 4-year span. In order to collect young children's narratives, Bloome, Champion and Katz developed a "storytelling project" which was conducted two times a week in a preschool and was The storytelling project was designed to elicit children's narratives in a variety of settings and in both spoken and written modes. The results suggested that children take up the narrative styles, structures, and content made available to them and then "experiment" with those styles, structures, and content. An example of a narrative collected by Bloome, Champion, and Katz ; see also Bloome, Champion, Katz, Morton and Muldrow (2001). The narrative is told by a four-year- old African American female named Sara.

1	C. This little
2	C. This little girl
3	C. was goin to the store to buy some candy
4	C. and when she was going to the store
5	C. when she got to the store
6	C. she say
7	C. why
8	C. Why don't I get some fruit to eat
9	C. to eat
10	C. den she got some fruit when she went to the fruit store
11	C. She say it was very good
12	C. but the fruit store I ask my mom can I have some more stuff
13	C. well she say
14	C. next morning she went to school and said
15	C. mom
16	C. can I ask you something
17	C. and mom said
18	C. yes dear
19	C. Well mom I need a couple books for my project
20	C. and she said
21	A. OK
22	C. and the mom went to the store and got her some books for the project
23	C. den that's the end
24	A. Allright very good excellent

Sara's story begins with a language form that signals a story, "This little girl was goin' to the store to go buy some candy." The story is not about her. Going to the store is a highly valued activity for all children as is buying candy. On line 6 Sara begins the use of Dailogue. The little girl no longer wants candy; now she wants some fruit. Perhaps Sara has picked up this line from her parents who may have told her to get some fruit instead of candy. Perhaps she is using the line here to redefine the little girl as someone more mature than a child who would get candy. The little girl in line 10 has gone to the fruit store. There are a small number of fruit stores in the city, so it is possible that she did indeed go to a fruit store. In line 12, at the fruit store, the story stops being about the little girl and switches into the first person. The story changes to being about Sara and her mom. The dialogue in lines 13 through 21 may be a repetition of a conversation she had with her mother or it may have been constructed from bits of conversation with her mother and with others. What it does show is that her mother is a responsible parent (see line 13 and the mother's response to being asked for more stuff), and that the child and her mother have a loving relationship (line 18). Moreover, the storyteller reveals that her mother will get her stuff if it is the right kind, such as items for school (line 19 and line 122) — which may be part of the moral of the story (fruit instead of candy, and books instead of stuff)–in addition to showing the loving relationship between herself and her mother.

Bloome, Champion and Katz (1997) analyzed the narrative based on the event of storytelling and not on the structure of the story. These findings challenge the notion that a narrative or storytelling itself must be evaluated solely or even primarily in terms of the structure of texts or textual events, as opposed to the role of the narrative and storytelling event in making a claim for particular social identities and social relationships.

Hester (1996) examined narratives of two African American fourth-grade students from a database of 60 African American children in an urban school setting. There were three different prompting tasks: having a conversation, retelling an event, and generating from pictures. Narratives were analyzed according to code-switching and style shifting. The following narrative is an excerpt of a conversation prompt from Hester's data.

Tisha, 4th grader

1   I: Tell me about your family

2   T: I got a grandmovuh.

3   She buy me a lot.

4   I like my movuh cause she do too.

5   I like my brovuh cause he [is] smart.

6   And I teach him how to read and stuff.

7   I: Tell me more about your brother.

8   T: He like reading.

9   Sometime, I read wif him.

10   But sometime, he just read by hisself

11   cause he know all the words.

12   I: How old is he?

13   T: Five.

14   I: He's really smart then. Did you teach him how to read?

15   T: He say, "Can I read your book?"

16. And I say, "You can't read my book because you're not old enough

17. to read the book that I read."

18   He say, "I can read it.

19   I: Was he able to read your book?

20   T: Some words he could, some words he couldn't. (p.233)

According to Hester (1996), Tisha's narrative contains both oral and literate features, but it is more consistent with the oral language style. Hester's analysis of orality includes the areas of syntax, cohesion, semantics and narrative structure. In the area of syntax, Tisha used direct quotes (lines 15 through 18), while in the area of cohesion she used additives and some causal markers (lines 4, 5, 11). Causal markers are used frequently in the literate tradition (Hester, 1996). In the area of semantics, Tisha used formulaic language and emphatic particles. Depending on the prompting task, Hester found oral and literate features.

Hyon and Sulzby (1994) examined the narrative styles of 48 African American kindergartners using Michael's (1981) topic associating and topic centered categories. Narrative accounts were elicited by adult interviewers with the child in a separate room from his/her classmates. The interviewer invited the child to tell a story. Results indicate that 16 children told topic associating accounts while 28 told topic centered narratives:

Steven

1   C. the house was fired up

2   C. then the fire truck came

3   C. then they had the water spray in there, and stop, and got burned-ed up

4   C. but it was up there to the house

5   C. it went up

6   C. it went over

7   C. and then it sprayed again and again

8   C. and they stay stayed over there that long

9   C. but they was go move their house

10   C. but this fire up, but it ain't burn no more

Hyon and Sulzby categorized Steven's narrative as topic centered. In his narrative, a single theme is emphasized: a house fire being extinguished. The narrative begins with an orientation, then moves on to the arrival of a fire truck. Next Steven recounts the fire being sprayed with the fire hose, and finally the fire being extinguished. Hyon and Sulzby found, like Steven's story, that African American kindergartners in their study produced more topic centered narratives than topic associating narratives.

Champion, Katz, Muldrow, and Dail (1999) examined narratives from African American pre-schoolers using content and event analyses. Both analyses were applied to the cultural and social knowledge underlying narrative production in the African American preschoolers. Here is an example of a narrative produced by a 4 =year=old African American male child using pictures he has drawn as prompts:

Mamadou

1.   C. This is a story about my mama pick me up from school

2.   C. This is a story about my mother comes to pick me up from school

3.   C. My grandmama

4.   C. My grandmama picking me up from school—right?

5   C. And she had to go all the way to the other street to pick me up

6   C. And there's my grandmama right there and there is me

This narrative was analyzed using both event and content analyses. The event analysis finds in line 1, Mamadou bids for the floor, and then initiates topic and interaction with the audience. In line 2, he maintains the interaction with his classmates. In addition, in lines 1 and 2, Mamadou repeats his opening twice. The repetition is also a form of parallelism, which signals a conversational tie between lines 1 and 2.

In lines 3 and 4, the main character shifts from mother to grandmother. Mamadou maintains interaction with the audience and is successful with the shift. Again, parallelism is used to signal links between statements. He also ends line 4 with the interrogative word "right," as a public confirmation for his statement about "my grandmama picking me up from school."

In line 5, Mamadou continues interaction with his audience by explaining that his grandmother had to go beyond what is expected of a family in picking up children from school. This statement may also serve as a suspense builder to keep the audience interested in his story. He also signals a temporal tie "and" to link the sequential nature of the content in lines 4 and 5. He again uses parallelism (pick me up) to link line 5 to lines 1 and 2. In lines 5 and 6 , Mamadou continues to link the statements together temporally by using "and" as a cohesive tie. Finally, in line 6 he ends the interaction and the story by showing a picture of his grandmother and himself. The patterns emerging from the event analysis show that Mamadou bids for the floor, and initiates topic and interaction with his audience. In addition, Mamadou produced cohesive devices that included parallelism and semantic ties. These results suggest that the use of alternative analysis may broaden the understanding of narrative structures among children.

Discourse Strategies within the African American Community

One cannot talk about narratives by African American children without commenting on discourse style within the African American community. This unique style of discourse is entrenched in the African American culture that has been passed on from generation to generation, despite the oppression of African Americans from slavery to the present day. Researchers such as Smitherman (1977), Burling (1973) and Kochman (1972) have examined African American oral tradition and found specific characteristics inherent to it.

Smitherman (1977) defines call-response as spontaneous verbal and nonverbal interaction between the speaker and the listener in which all of the speaker's statements (calls) are punctuated by expressions (responses) from the listener (p. 104). This communication process is often heard in the traditional Black church, but it is not limited to the church. I offer an example of call-response that comes from personal experience: One day, as my mother was telling me a story about a neighbor who was sick and got a ride home from a stranger, I interjected, "God is good." She replied, "all the time" and then continued the story (Champion, 1999).

Burling (1973) defines signifying as teasing or taunting speech " . . . used most specifically for language that goads another into performing an aggressive act" (p. 85). An excellent example of signifying is the "Signifyin' Monkey" by Oscar Brown, Jr. (Goss & Barnes, 1989):

Said the signifyin' monkey to the lion one day:

'Hey, dere's a great big elephant down th' way

Goin' 'roun' talkin', I'm sorry t' say,

About yo' momma in a scandalous way!

'Yea, he's talkin' 'bout yo' momma an' yo grandma, too;

And he don' show too much respect fo' you.

Now, you weren't there an' I sho' am glad

'Cause what he said about yo' momma made me mad!'. . . . (p. 456)

In this narrative, the monkey goads the lion into a fight with the elephant by signifying or indicating that the elephant has been insulting the lion.

The term *dozens* is a form of signification with the verbal insults on family members, often the mother, instead of insulting the person directly. Smitherman (1977) states that the most common specific verbalism of the dozens is the simple retort "Yo *momma*." Kochman, in his book, *Toward an Ethnography of Black American Speech Behavior* (1972), uses the term *sounding* to classify the game of verbal insult known as the dozens. Kochman writes:

> In Chicago, the term *sounding* would describe the initial remarks which are designed to sound out the person to see whether he will play the game. The verbal insult is also subdivided, the term signifying applying to those insults which are hurled directly at the person and the dozens applying to insults hurled at an opponent's family, especially the mother. (p. 258)

Kochman gives the following example: "I walked in your house and your family was running around the table. I said, 'Why you doin that?' Your momma say, 'First one drops, we eat" (p. 261).

Another oral tradition is narrative sequencing. Smitherman (1977) defines narrative sequencing as storytelling that is often associated with toasts and other kinds of folklore in the African American community. Examples of narrative sequencing typically occur within preaching, personal storytelling (narrative renditions of situations that occur in life), and toasts (a toast can be story such as "The Signifyin' Monkey") . Table 2.3 lists some of the features of African American oral traditions.

TABLE 2.3 An Abbreviated Table of Features of the African American Oral Tradition

FEATURES
Call-response — Spontaneous verbal interactions between speaker and listener.
Signifying — Teasing or taunting speech.
Dozens or Sounding — Form of signifying with insults on family members.
Narrative Sequencing can be divided into at least five areas: Toasts Personal Storytelling Folktales Ghost Stories Preaching

The oral tradition that is entrenched in the African American culture has been passed on from generation to generation in large part because slavery prohibited teaching African Americans to read and write. In addition to the oral tradition, however, Africans have a long literate tradition, with inscriptions found on sacred Egyptian texts. The alphabet originated with Africans, and writing among religious leaders was prominent (Dandy, 1991).

Narrative Strategies Within West Africa

The spoken word is very important within African culture. Isidore Okpewho, in his book *African Oral Literature* (1992), details nine stylistic characteristics of oral storytelling within Africa. The first stylistic characteristic is repetition, which he defined as the narrator using the same key phrases throughout the narrative. Awona (1966, cited in Okpewho, 1992) presents an example of repetition: "Dashed like the branch of a broken tree,/ Like the furious racing of a young antelope,/ Like a bird that takes off without saying goodbye to the branch" (p. 76). This formula is used seven times in the narrative. Okpewho observes that the oral performance (whether song or story) relies heavily on these repeated devices not only to achieve a rhythmic effect that appeals both to the audience and to the performer, but also to support the overall framework on which the performance is built. Hence, it can be said that repetition is a distinguishing feature of oral literature (pp. 77- 78).

The second stylistic characteristic of African oral literature is <u>parallelism</u>, which Okpewho defines as the use of identical words that are transposed within the same or adjacent statements. In a narrative by Beir and Gbadamosi (1959, cited in Okpewho 1992) illustrates the use of parallelism:

20   One day Onikoyi went out to rob.

Then a thief broke into his own house.

Onikoyi met the thief on the road.

The thief said, "Ha—is that not Onikoyi?"

Onikoyi said, "Ha-is that not the thief?"

25   They pounce on each other:

Onikoyi cuts off the thief's head.

The thief cries, 'Oshun, Sonponna, help me!'

Onikoyi replies, 'Whether you call Oshun or whether you call Sonponna

I am the one who cuts off the head; for every warrior is a bit of a Thief' (p. 80).

In lines 20 and 21 Onikoyi and the thief are robbing each other, illustrating both lexical and semantic parallelism in the narrative. In lines 23 and 24, the narrator uses lexical stylistic parallelism. Okpewho states that parallelism is frequently used in longer narratives due to the storyteller's memory loss. The narrator will use his imagination to play one set of words or images against another without changing the theme of the narrative.

The next stylistic characteristic is piling and association. Okpewho (1992) defines <u>piling and association</u> as heaping one detail onto another to build the narrative up to a climax. An example illustrating this style is seen in the following passage: "He who armed in the forest who is like a madman/ The madman who is in full view of men Cope, (1968, 72, cited in Okpewho, 1992). In this example, the narrator ends one statement with the word *"madman"* and begins the next statement with the same word , *"madman,"* Again, Okpewho proposes that the narrator is relying on his imagination to add to the story.

Tonality is another stylistic characteristic used in narratives. The narrator changes intonation throughout the story, especially in the last syllable of a line. This use of intonation contours to the rhythm of the narrative. An example taken from Yoruba by Lasebikan, (1955, 36, cited in Okpewho 1992) is

"'Ija` kan, i`ji` ka`n ti nwon ja` Lofa` nko'-

Oju' tal p' die m'be?" (p. 90).

In this passage we can see that the narrator uses low tones throughout the first line until the last syllable. In the next line, he uses high tones. While tonality varies from language to language, it is widely used across the African continent.

Ideophones are related to tonality by using sound to convey meaning. Okpewho (1992, p. 92) defined ideophones as "idea-in-sound." He states that ideophones are used in the production of narratives to add vividness and drama to the storytelling event.

Digression has been defined by Okpewho as a departure from the main theme of a narrative to address an object or person at the storytelling event or to comment on an issue related in some way to the theme of the narrative. We see an example of digression in the following passage by Innes, (1974, 281-82 cited in Okpewho, 1992):

They said, 'Let us take as provisions groundnuts,

And bitter tomatoes and okra and maize.'

That is what made those four things so loved by the Mandinka.

Before you cook oily food for a Mandinka elder,

Cook groundnuts for him—that is what he likes.

When a Mandinka man grows old, he likes to grow a parch of okra.

In any Mandinka town you go to,

You will find in it a garden growing maize.

They came and put down the three little piles of goods in the market.

Markets have been in existence for a very long time.

You know yourself, Seni Darbo, that even if you are in Europe.

When you see something from your own country in the market

That is the first thing you will buy. (p. 97)

Imagery, allusion, and symbolism, the last three stylistic characteristics have been discussed by other researchers (Gumperz, 1982; Tannen, 1989) in regards to written literature. Okpewho describes imagery as the use of words to paint mental pictures that appeal to our feelings and understanding. Two ways in which this is done is through similes and metaphors. A simile is a comparison achieved by indirect reference while a metaphor is a direct reference. An example of a metaphor by Deng, (1973, 192, cited in Okpewho, 1992) is in the sentence "The old man of the leopard world" (p. 120). "Old man" is directly referred to as a leopard in this sentence, thereby setting up the use of a metaphor.

Allusion uses images and ideas from real experience or from imaginative literature such as folktales. Okpewho offers an example of allusion with the billy goat that has taken over the tortoise's burden of death. Okpewho notes that this allusion, which stems from a folktale of the Asaba Igbo of Southwestern Nigeria, is commonly used to describe a generous act which lands the doer in trouble.

Symbolism is a concrete or a familiar object that is used as an explanation of an abstract idea or a less familiar object or event. The divination poetry of the Yoruba employs stories as parables, using highly symbolic language to explain problems.

Table 2.4 lists some of the features of West African narrative strategies.

TABLE 2.4 West African Narrative Strategies as discussed by Okpewho (1992)

STYLISTIC CHARACTERISTICS
Repetition — Narrator uses the same key phrases throughout the narrative.
Parallelism — The use of identical words that are transposed within the same or adjacent statements.
Piling and Association — Heaping one detail onto another to build the narrative into a climax.
Tonality — Intonation changes throughout the narrative.
Ideophone — Using sound to convey meaning.
Digression — A departure from the main theme of a narrative to address or comment to a person or object related to the theme of the narrative
Imagery — Defined as using words (similes and metaphors) to create images in the mind of the listener.
Allusion — An image used to convey meaning when the origin of the image is not verbally apparent
Symbolism — Defined as the use of a familiar image to convey lessons to the listener (i.e., animal folktales).

Purpose of Storytelling in West Africa

In his study on oral literature, Okpewho discusses four reasons for storytelling: to provide entertainment and relaxation, to assert interests and outlooks, to teach ideals and conduct, and to record life.

An example by Scheub, (1974, cited in Okpewho, 1992) illustrates how storytelling is used as a relaxation tool to release tension after a long day's work:

> For the evening storytelling session, we go to a compound in a ward
> of Ibadan where we find an extended family. . . . After the evening
> meal, the members of the family gather on a porch and if there is

moonlight, the younger members gather in the courtyard to play
games like hide and seek. On the porch, the entertainment begins
with riddles . . . . After a few riddles, the tales begin. (p. 165)

As the narrator tells the story, he accompanies it with various paralinguistic
devices such as gestures and head movement. Meanwhile, the audience identifies
with the plights of the characters, or at least adopts a critical attitude toward their
behaviors.

The second and third reasons for storytelling are closely tied to each other. In
asserting one's interests and outlooks, individuals come to terms with the world in
which they live. For example, each community has a story about the beginning of
civilization that is unique to that community. These and other types of stories provide a collective sense of who these people are, and help them define or compre-
hend the world at large in terms both familiar and positive to them. These narratives, which can be delivered either privately or publicly, contain important information for teaching ideals and conduct. An example of one type of narrative is the
animal trickster tale, which is designed to teach lessons on specific conduct or
behavior that should or should not be used by the audience. The final reason for
storytelling is to record historical events (birth, marriage, and death) among members of a particular community.

Summary

In summary, the first area of this chapter, a discussion of research focusing on
narrative production among African American children was reported. The
research findings centered on what type of narrative structures are produced by
African American children. Early research (Michaels, 1981) indicates that
African American children produced narrative structures that were found in their
communities. More recent research suggests that not only does culture shape narrative structure, but it affects social context and prompting tasks as well.
Collectively, these studies suggest that African American children produce a
repertoire of narrative structures.

The second area of the chapter focused on the oral tradition within the African
American community. A discussion of specific oral characteristics found in discourse was presented. The narrative features outlined in this text are call-response,
signifying and dozens. In addition, a discussion of the use narration in the African
American community was offered. It was noted that narrative sequencing can be
divided into least five categories: toasts, personal storytelling, folktales, ghost stories and preaching.

The last area of the chapter focused on the oral tradition within West Africa. Research was reported by Okpewho (1992) who studied oral narratives in West Africa. He reported nine stylistic characteristics used in oral narratives: repetition, parallelism, tonality, ideophones, piling and association, digression, imagery, allusion and symbolism. In addition, Okpewho (1992), stated the reasons for narrating were for relaxation, teaching, and recording historical events.

These three areas form the background information necessary for understanding narrative structures among African American children today. The next chapter focuses on how the research reported in this chapter has been extended to study a group of African American children.

3
Extending the Research: A Study of Narrative Production Among African American Children

This book builds upon and extends the research on narrative production among African American children. This study incorporates a mixed research design integrating qualitative and quantitative methodology. The research methodology for this book was influenced by the ethnography of communication and the ethnographic study of ways of speaking and using language. In addition, I used experimental procedures to elicit the narratives from the children in the study were implemented.

Fifteen African American children, between the ages of 6 and 10 years, from a predominantly African American low-income community in the northeastern United States participated in the study. Table 3.1 lists the participants by age and sex.

TABLE 3.1 Participants' Profiles by Sex and Age

Child	Sex	Age
TYW	M	6.9
JOT	M	7.0
SYG	F	7.0
SHR	F	7.1
LAI	F	7.5
TIB	F	8.2
CHW	F	8.3
RER	F	8.5
TIR	F	8.7
RAR	M	9.5
DEC	F	9.5
FRF	F	9.8
SES	M	9.9
LEW	F	10.7
MAJ	M	10.9

The data were collected in the after school programs held at two community centers. The first site was the St. Paul Community Center in Springfield, Massachusetts. This community center was started in 1991 by members of the St. Paul A.M.E. church to meet the needs of its members and of the community at large. Since the program is secular, it has no religious affiliation to the church. The second site used for this study was the Fannie Lou Hamer Community Center, a mile away from the St. Paul Community Center.

In order to participate in the study, children had to speak AAE. Two listening tasks were used to identify AAE speakers. One listening task involved a 5-minute audiotaped segment from each child's language sample that was rated by two African American judges in order to determine each child's status as an AAE speaker. Both judges the examiner and one other person were PhD graduate students who were familiar with characteristics of AAE. Graduate student judges lived in an African American community and had taken at least one course focusing on AAE. Both judges were asked to identify features commonly used by AAE speakers. The investigator selected 10 phonological and 18 syntactic characteristics of AAE for this purpose (see Appendix B). These characteristics were selected because they are most commonly used by AAE speakers. For children to be considered AAE speakers, a minimum of two phonological and/or three grammatical features needed to be identified by the judges. Table 3.2 provides a profile by each participant. For the second listening task, the investigator observed participants in various activities.

TABLE 3.2 Ratings of Participants' AAE Phonological and/or Grammatical Features

Participants	Judge 1	Judge 2
TYW	8	7
JOT	3	3
SYG	4	0
SHR	5	4
LAI	6	3
TIB	3	5
CHW	4	4
RER	3	4
TIR	7	8
RAR	4	3
DEC	4	4
FRF	1	4
SES	5	4
LEW	1	5
MAJ	4	4

In the second listening task special attention was devoted to LEW, SYG, and FRF because they did not meet the first requirement for identification. Within their various activities, especially in free play with peer groups, these participants produced the minimum number of features as identified in task 1 for inclusion in the study. The selection criteria for LEW, SYG, and FRF were verified by the second judge. Both Listening Task 1 and Listening Task 2 served to identify AAE child speakers. Table 3.3 presents an abbreviated list of African American English features. Please see Appendix B for a detailed description of AAE features.

TABLE 3.3 An abbreviated list of African American English (AAE) features.

AAE FEATURES	EXAMPLES
PHONOLOGY	
1. Reduction of a Final Consonant of a Consonant Cluster.	
(a) when both consonants of a cluster belong to the same word (usually applies when both members of the cluster are either voiced or voiceless)	best → bes,
	band → ban
	robbed → rob,
(b) when past tense {-ed} is added to a word	kissed → kis
(c) when a word beginning with a vowel follows a word- final consonant cluster, the final consonant of the cluster may be omitted	best apple → bes apple
2. Production of / / and /O/.	
(a) The voiced interdental fricative / th / may be pronounced as [d] when in the initial word position	this → dis
(b) The voiceless interdental fricative (/O/), may be produced as a [t].	thin → tin.
3. Production of /r/ and /l/.	
(a) The /r/ and /l/ may be substituted by an unstressed schwa.	sistuh → sister;
	steal → steauh
(b) omission of the /r/ and /l/ when they precede a consonant in a word.	horse → ho's
(c) omission of the /r/ and /l/ when they follow an /o/ or/u/.	carol → ca'ol.

4. Devoicing of Final /b/, /d/, and /g/. In word-final positions, /b/, /d/, and /g/, may be produced as [p], [t], and [k].	pig → p::ik; lid → l::it; lab → l::ap
5. Vowel Glide Production. Vowels that precede a voiceless consonant may be produced with a glide.	kite → k::ite; flight → fl::ight
6. Nasalization. The final nasal consonant in the word-final position may be deleted, but the preceding vowel sounds may have a nasalized quality.	Nasalization of vowels preceding nasals produce homophones in words such as rum, run and rung.

SYNTAX

1. Deletion of {ed} Suffix. Because of the consonant reduction rule discussed under phonology, the {ed} marking for past tense, past participles forms, and derived adjectives are affected.	They talked yesterday → They talk yesterday; He has finished the job → He has finish the job; She is a blue-eyed baby → She is a blue-eye baby.
2. The Regularization of Irregular Verbs. The {ed} marker may be added to those present tense form of verbs that should have an irregular past tense.	He ran home → He runned home.
3. Deletion of Forms of Have. The auxiliary have may be contracted to form 've and 's; However, in AAE these contractions may be deleted in the present tense.	She's done well → She done well; They've gotten together → They gotten together.

4. **Deletion of {s} Suffix in Third Person Subject Verb Agreement.** The {s} suffix marker may be deleted in the present tense of verbs when the subject of those verbs is in the third person singular.	He bakes a cake ➔ He bake a cake.
5. **Deletion of Third Person Singular Forms of Have and Do.** In Standard English, have and do become has and does in third person singular subject constructions. This change may not take place in AAE.	He has two coins ➔ He have two coins; She does many tricks ➔ She do many tricks.
6. **Deletion of {-s} Suffix Plural Marker.** When nouns are classified by a plural quantifier, the {-s} plural marker may be deleted.	The boy has five apples ➔ The boy has five apple.
7. **Deletion of {-s} Suffix Possessive Marker.** The {-s} marker may be deleted in possessive-word relations.	Bill's hat ➔ Bill hat.
8. **Deletion of Contracted Form of Will.** There are two conditions under which the future indicator (will) may be deleted: (a) when it is contracted, (b) when it precedes a word that begins with a labial consonant.	a) I'll follow the train ➔ I follow the train. b) I will be quick about it - ➔ I be quick about it.

9. **Invariant Be Form of the Verb To Be.** The form be may be used as a main verb and can refer to either habitual or intermittent action as opposed to a single event.	He is writing ➜ He be writing.
10. **Deletion of Contracted Is and Are.** Wherever is and are can be contracted in Standard English, they may be deleted in AAE.	She's pretty ➜ She pretty; They're bold ➜ They bold.
11. **Multiple Negation.** There are several ways in which negation is expressed in AAE: a) the addition of two negatives to an auxiliary b) two negatives added in the case of converting an indefinite to a negative form, c) two negatives added to did.	a) I can't go ➜ I can't never go. b) I am somebody ➜ I am not nobody (I ain't nobody). c) I did not do anything ➜ I ain't did nothing.

Note: Table 3.2 is adapted from work of Wolfram and Fasold (1974) and Seymour, Champion and Jackson (1995).

Data Transcription, and Reliability

All subject utterances were transcribed using standard orthography and, when necessary, phonetic (IPA symbol) transcription procedures. Once narratives were transcribed, 20% of the narratives were checked for reliability. The investigator served as judge for broad transcription. There was 96% reliability for broad transcription.

Next, each narrative was coded from broad transcription using evaluative analysis (Labov, 1972; Peterson & McCabe, 1983) and episodic analysis (Peterson & McCabe, 1983). Once narratives were coded, 20% of the narratives were checked for reliability.

Narrative Data Collection Process

Narratives were elicited by engaging each subject in a conversation. This method is based on Peterson and McCabe's (1983) study of 96 children, ages 3½ to 9½ years. The Peterson and McCabe method was chosen because of its naturalist formula of engaging the child in conversation. Conversation topics were derived from short stories told by the investigator. Children were given a choice of toys as well as a choice of coloring books. The toys consisted of a pool table, a basketball game, and four African American dolls with a change of clothing; the coloring books were *Aladdin*, *Barney and Baby Bop*, and *Barbie*. The toys were chosen because during practice sessions with the camera, children were not talkative until a play session with toys was initiated.

Below is a list of stories that were used as prompts with all children:

1. Grandma/trouble. When I was younger, I used to go down South every summer to visit my grandmother, who lived on a farm. One time my brother and I went to the chicken coop to feed the chickens and we let them out by mistake. The chickens went all over the yard. My grandmother yelled at us for letting the chickens out.

2. Stitches/hospital. When I was younger, my brother and I were down South visiting my aunt. My brother climbed a tree in the backyard and fell out of the tree onto a wagon. He hurt his leg and had to go to the hospital to get stitches.

3. Baby sibling. I used to play with my friend Audrey when I was younger. One day, when we were playing outside we were chased by some boys on the block. We ran inside my apartment, where my little baby brother was sleeping. When we ran in we woke him up and he started crying. My aunt came into the room and said, "You woke him up. You put him back to sleep."

The same follow-up question was asked after each story was told: "Did anything like that ever happen to you or someone you know?" If the response was yes, a second follow-up question was asked.

An additional type of prompt was used because of the possibility that the story prompts did not appeal to some, or all of the children. The prompting went as follows: "Tell me a time when you were. . .":

1.	a hero	5.	having a hard time
2.	a helper	6.	funny
3.	scared	7.	sick
4.	angry		

Data Analysis

I performed a multi-step analysis of narratives produced by the participants in this study. Each step of the different analyses is described.

Evaluative Analysis

There are seven narrative structures in the evaluative analysis. The first structure is very similar to Labov's (1972) definition of a well-formed narrative, which consists of an orientation, complicating action, evaluation and a resolution. Peterson and McCabe (1983) refer to this as the "classic" structure. The remaining six structures (ending-at-the-highpoint, leapfrogging, the chronological form, the impoverished form, the disoriented structure, and the miscellaneous structure) were developed by Peterson and McCabe.

Labov (1972) developed the classic structure when he worked with African American English speaking children and adolescents. He defined it as "a complete narrative [which] begins with an orientation, proceeds to the complicating action, is suspended at the focus of the evaluation before the resolution, concludes with resolution, and returns the listener to the present with the coda" (p. 369). In the classic structure, the narrator leads up to the evaluative mode where the action is suspended. During this suspension, the narrative is evaluated before the result or resolution is given. After the evaluation, the narrator resolves the situation. Children use this structure with increasing success as they age.

The second structure is called ending-at-the-highpoint (Peterson & McCabe, 1983). The narrator presents a series of events leading up to the complicating action. The highpoint is reached, but there is no resolution. Some storytellers will use this structure to give a surprise ending, such as in ghost stories. Peterson and McCabe suggest that children who use ending-at-the-highpoint structure are approximating the classic structure, but ending the stories too soon. This structure is common with children 5 to 6 years old and decreases in frequency with older children. According to Peterson and McCabe, children at this stage are moving toward the classic structure.

The third structure is called leapfrogging. Peterson and McCabe (1983) described this and the remaining narrative structures as being primitive forms of narration. In the leapfrogging structure children jump from one event to another, omitting information and making it difficult for the listener to understand the narrative. This structure is common with children who are 4 years old and starts to decrease when children are around 4 1/2 years old.

The next structure is the chronological structure, which is temporally integrated (Peterson & McCabe, 1983). In this form, children may provide a list of events that have occurred. A chronological narrative does not have an evaluative mode. The chronological structure is common among children who are 4 years old. If the child is not interested or involved in telling the narrative, a chronological structure may occur at any age.

The impoverished narrative is the fifth structure (Peterson & McCabe, 1983). In these narratives children use a few sentences that are hard to analyze. In some cases, "they provide two successive events, and then go over and over them, often providing extensive orientation and evaluation about these two events" (p. 45). The impoverished narrative structure is common with 4 –year- olds.

The disoriented narrative is the sixth structure (Peterson & McCabe, 1983). Children who use this structure are either confused or disoriented about the action depicted in the narrative and therefore the narrative cannot be understood by the listener. This rare structure is most frequently observed with 4-year -old children.

The last structure is the miscellaneous structure—a term applied to narratives that do not fit any of the preceding patterns. Peterson and McCabe (1983) did report, however, that most children's narratives will fit the other patterns mentioned. The miscellaneous structure can occur at any age.

The three structures occurring most often among children are leapfrogging, ending-at-the-highpoint, and the classic structure. Children must pass through developmental stages to achieve what Labov (1972) calls the most sophisticated structure, the classic form. Peterson and McCabe (1983) have shown that narratives at different stages can be analyzed while still employing Labov's framework. Children ages 3 1/2 to 9 1/2 may use different narrative structures yet have the same goal as the classic structure. These patterns— the miscellaneous structure, the disoriented structure, the impoverished structure, the chronological structure, the leapfrogging structure, ending-at-highpoint, and the classic structure— are ordered from the least complex to the most complex form.

Each narrative clause was coded for one of the following: orientation, complicating action, resolution, evaluation, or appendages. Twenty percent of narratives were judged for reliability at 87% accuracy. Narrative clauses were also coded for the subcategories. Each narrative was then coded by its structural pattern (classic, ending-at-highpoint, leapfrogging, chronological, impoverished, disoriented, and miscellaneous pattern). For reliability purposes 20% of narratives were coded independently, with 85% reliability achieved. Each structure was analyzed for proportional frequency across age groups.

Episodic Analysis

Glenn and Stein (1980) found seven major types of story structures: descriptive sequences, action sequences, reactive sequences, abbreviated episodes, complete episodes, complex episodes, and interactive episodes. These structures are classified from least complex to the most complex form. Each structure includes all categories of statements and functions, and the relationships between the categories.

The earliest structures to develop are classified as sequences, which have been defined as a series of statements that may not be causally related. The first sequence is called a descriptive sequence. Descriptive sequences are simple descriptions of setting, character, and actions. Categories in this sequence may include external and internal states, natural occurrences, and the actions of the character.

The action sequence focuses on the character's behaviors; actions may or may not be accompanied by external and internal states and natural occurrences. These statements are logically ordered and temporally joined.

The reactive sequence reflects changes in the character's environment. One event causes another event to happen. This sequence is not based on content, but relies on functions within the narrative. Categories in this sequence include events, reactions, and settings. These three sequences represent the least complex structures in narratives. Typically, young children use these sequences (Glenn & Stein, 1980).

In episodes, there is some requirement of causal relationship and planning by the characters in the narrative. Episodes can be classified as being abbreviated, complete, complex, and interactive; this taxonomy ranges in complexity from least to most complex.

In an abbreviated episode, the main character's (or protagonist's) goals are to be inferred because they are not explicitly stated. There is a motive for action which is represented by an internal state or an event. This event will lead to a consequence. The consequence will lead to the achievement of, or the failure to achieve, the protagonist's goal.

The complete episode shares the abbreviated episode's characteristics; however, in this episode, there is more evidence of internal planning by the protagonist. Categories included in this episode are motivating states, attempts, and consequences. The consequences are obligatory and cannot be omitted. Optional categories are settings and reactions.

The complex episode is divided into four categories. In the first type, one structure can function as a single unit in a higher order. For example, a reactive sequence can trigger a response from the protagonist. In the second type, a complete episode functions as a single unit. The third and fourth structures involve some type of complication in the pursuit of the goal. A plan application may be repeated if the first attempt to reach a goal has failed. In the fourth structure, not only is the plan repeated, but there may also be an embedded episode.

The fourth episode has been described as being interactive in that it involves two people with goals that influence each other. Statements by each individual serve many functions within this episode.

Each narrative clause or sentence was coded as an event, motivating states attempt, consequence, reactions, setting, judgment, and appendage. Twenty percent of narratives were coded independently with 85% reliability. Second, each narrative was coded by seven major types of story structures (Glenn & Stein, 1980): descriptive sequences, action sequences, reactive sequences, abbreviated episodes, complete episodes, complex episodes, and interactive episodes. Twenty percent of narratives were coded independently with 87% reliability. All structures and relationships were analyzed for proportional frequency across age groups.

To summarize, both episodic and evaluative analyses use a priori taxonomy in which children's narrative production are categorized from least to most complex. Episodic analysis has been used widely within the field of speech language pathology to assess children's ability to produce narratives that follow a linear pattern (from beginning to middle to end, Lahey, 1988). One assumption underlying episodic analysis is that narratives have some kind of internal structure similar to sentences (Rumelhart, 1975). For a child's narrative skills to be fully developed, he or she must approximate a linear structure (Rumelhart, 1975).

Thematic Analysis

A thematic analysis identifies recurring elements of a cultural phenomena. Thematic analysis was used to identify the interactional function of narratives produced by children. Spradley's (1980) procedures for thematic analysis guided the procedures used in this study. First, the narratives were reviewed until they became familiar. Next, videotapes of the narratives were studied to examine their nonverbal and paralinguistic features. Narratives were initially categorized by sorting them according to the prompts used for elicitation. Similar patterns of themes emerged across all categories. Patterns of themes were then listed from the data and the data were sorted by these thematic patterns.

Sociolinguistic Analysis

The videotaped narratives were analyzed to obtain sociolinguistic factors. Two steps were involved, making a transcript and describing utterances.

Making a Transcript

A transcript was developed to systematically describe the structure and cohesion of narratives produced by the children. Not all narratives were transcribed; only narratives that did not fit in the higher end of a priori evaluative and episodic analyses were developed into transcripts. Transcript analysis was based on how the utterances related to each other. Utterances could be tied to each other by prosody, nonverbal behavior, semantic cohesive ties, or parallelism. Transcript analysis has been influenced by Gumperz's (1982) work on prosody and Pierrehumbert's (1980) work on intonation.

The first step in this analysis was to transcribe the narrative. A line-by-line, detailed description of prosodic features was provided with the intonation analysis based on Pierrehumbert (1980). There are tonal units that are understood abstractly as High or Low. With this model one can have pitch accents which are synonymous with a stressed syllable (H*). One can also have boundary tones that are realized around either the initial or final syllable of an intonational phrase. There was 100% reliability agreement of the transcript; the investigator and fellow researcher worked on the case concurrently and resolved any disagreements as they occurred. For the purposes of this study, the descriptive level of analysis to examine prosody with a sociolinguistic framework was used. The audiotaped version of the narrative was transferred to the WAVES program on the Sun computer to analyze fundamental frequency and to check auditory perception of the intonational pattern of the narrative. Other contextualization cues (Gumperz, 1982) included verbal, nonverbal, and prosodic. Nonverbal cues were included in the transcript and verbal utterances by the narrator and investigator were written out verbatim.

Description of Utterances

Describing the function of prosody in the narratives entailed three parts. Modified descriptive system was taken from Bloome (1989). Utterances were transcribed five different ways: source, social interaction, function, form and cohesive ties. The source description in the transcript indicates who is talking or initiating an event. The social interaction function describes the purpose or use of an utterance within the narrative, and is used to describe the development of social relationships (Bloome, 1989). Functions include initiating interaction, initiating topic, requesting, informing expressing judgment, agreeing, bidding for the floor, maintaining interaction, ending, and shifting topic. Utterance form is described as a question, statement, or response. Cohesive ties describe endophoric and exophoric cohesive links between utterances and events occurring during their production.

The next step was examining the meaning/function of the cohesive ties. It is the contention of the writer that the speaker signals cohesion (Bloome, 1989; Gumperz, 1982) with sociolinguistic contextual cues.

The final of step of the sociolinguistic analysis was to examine features found within West African storytelling. Please refer back to chapter 2 for a discussion of narrative strategies discussed by Okpewho (1992).

Summary

To summarize, this chapter discusses the research design and methodology used for the study. Fifteen African American children who were speakers of AAE who participated in the study. A limited review of AAE features was presented. (See Appendix B for a full description of linguistic features of AAE). The narratives were elicited by engaging the children in conversation. Two types of prompts were used to elicit narratives: story and "Tell me a time when _____." Data analyses of the narratives consisted of: evaluative, episodic, thematic and sociolinguistic. The first two analyses are traditional and are used frequently in schools for evaluation. The third analysis takes into account the child's culture, and the last analysis examined narrative strategies used in West African oral narratives. Part II of the book reports the results from the evaluative, episodic, thematic and sociolinguistic analyses.

PART II
Toward a Repertoire of Narrative Structures Among African American Children

The purpose of this part II of the book is to provide evidence that African American children produce a repertoire of narrative structures that are complex in nature. The narratives that were produced by the children in this study suggest speculatively that they may be linked to African American culture, and possibly to West African culture.

In the following chapters, I present four different analyses. Although it would appear that the results should be parallel, they are not, because the analyses focus on different elements within the narratives. In the first two chapters (Chapters 4 and 5), evaluative and episodic analyses are presented. Both of these approaches are a priori and consider elements within the narratives. Analyzing narratives for only their linear structure may tend to identify "deficits" or "what's missing" in children. A narrative analysis must go beyond examining the structural coherence of a text. For a broader interpretation of a narrative, it is important that children's cultural and social practices be taken into account (Champion, 1998; Champion, Katz, Muldrow & Dail, 1999).

By viewing narratives as a social practice, one can examine how narrators not only tell about the past, but also negotiate present and future events. When examining the contexts in which narrators tell particular narratives to particular listeners, one must take a different position than simply one that rests on an a priori, hierarchical scheme such as the one reflected in the evaluative and episodic analyses where, for example, leapfrogging and the reactive sequence are on the lower end of the hierarchical scheme.

Previous findings in the leapfrogging and reactive categories has led me to consider using thematic and sociolinguistic analyses. Within the sociolinguistic analysis, I also examined the children's narratives by comparing them to discourse strategies and structures traditionally found in African and African American communities.

The first two chapters of Part II examine narratives using two traditional psycholinguistic analyses. In chapter 4, results are reported using evaluative analysis. The participants in this study produced the classic structure most frequently. In chapter 5, the episodic analysis yielded similar results, with complex structures being produced most often.. Chapter 6 presents results using thematic and some aspects of West African narrative strategies to analyze narratives. These narratives have been coded as "moral centered." In chapter 7, narratives are coded as "performative" using thematic and sociolinguistic analyses.

4
Evaluative Narratives

Participants ranged from 6 to 10 years old. For purpose of the evaluative and episodic analyses, participants were divided into three groups: Group 1, ages 6.9 to 7.5 years; Group 2, ages 8.2 to 8.7 years; and Group 3, ages 9.5 to 10.9 years. Table 4.1 provides a participant profile by age and sex.

TABLE 4.1

Participants' Profiles by Sex and Age

Participant	Sex	Age
GROUP 1		
TYW	M	6.9
JOT	M	7.0
SYG	F	7.0
SHR	F	7.1
LAI	F	7.5
GROUP 2		
TIB	F	8.2
CHW	F	8.3
RER	F	8.5
TIR	F	8.7
GROUP 3		
RAR	M	9.5
DEC	F	9.5
FRF	F	9.8
SES	M	9.9
LEW	F	10.7
MAJ	M	10.9

There were a total of 71 narratives. All the narratives produced were analyzed using evaluative analysis. Seven structural patterns were analyzed: the classic, ending-at-the-highpoint, leapfrogging, chronological, impoverished, disoriented, and miscellaneous. The results are presented on two levels: the overall production of patterns, and the production of structures within each group.

Overall Production of Structures

In order of prevalence, from most prevalent to least prevalent, the structures the narratives followed were the classic structure, the chronological structure, the leapfrogging structure, the ending-at- the-highpoint structure, and the impoverished structure.

Classic Structure

Labov and Waletzky (1967) defined the classic structure.

A simple sequence of complication and result does not indicate to a listener the relative importance of these events or help him distinguish complication from resolution. . . . Therefore it is necessary for the narrator to delineate the structure of the narrative by emphasizing the point where the complication has reached a maximum: the break between the complication and the result. (pp. 34-35)

Forty-seven narratives, or 66%, were classified as classic. A narrative example using the stitches/hospital prompt is presented:

Stitches/hospital

1. A. Have you ever had to get stitches?
2. C. no, but my little brother
3. C. he, um, he was real young
4. C. I think he was two years old
5. C. an' my mother was drivin'
6. C. an' my my uncle was in fron' seat
7. C. an' me an' my younger cousin dat lives in Baltimore, she's eight years old
8. C. her name is Whitney
9. C. an' my little brother was sittin' next to us
10 C. an' we was lookin' aroun'
11. C. an' he started playin' with da door
12. C. an' the door was unlocked

13.   C. an' he opened the door an' he fell out the car

14.   C. an' he was he was flippin' back

15.   C. an' he his head was busted open an' he had da
       get stitches

16.   C. an' me an my cousin Whitney was sittin' in the back o'
       the car cryin' because he fell out the car

17.   C. my mother kep' goin'

18.   C. an he did then my uncle Al said, "Rhonda stop the car"
       because he fell out the car

19.   C. an' she got out the car

20.   C. and, she was actin' crazy

21.   C. an' she got 'im

22.   C. an' we took 'im to the hospital

23.   A. what do you mean she was actin' crazy?

24.   C. like she like OH MY GOD she like MY BABY

25.   A. so you took him to the hospital and what happened?

26.   C. and he got a cast around his head

27.   C. an' den, he got stitches an' we brought him home

In this narrative, lines 2-8 serve as the orientation. The characters in the narrative are introduced in lines 2, 5, 6 and 7. In lines 3, 4, 7, 8 more information is given about the characters (the brother is 2 years old and a girl cousin named Whitney who lives in Baltimore is 8 years old). The place (riding in a car) is also in lines 5, 6 and 9. Lines 10-14 represent the complicating action of the child playing with the lock, who later falls out of the car. Lines 21, 22, 26 and 27 are the results of the complicating action (She got him and we went to the hospital). The end of line 27 serves as a coda. Lines 14-20, we are held in suspense, waiting for result of the child falling out of the car. These lines are full of evaluative statements such as line 18 (Rhonda, stop the car); direct statement, symbolic action in lines 16 and 20 (She was acting crazy) and figurative language line 14 (He was flipping back). This narrative, which has the elements of orientation, complicating action, evaluation, resolution and coda, has been defined as a classic form.

Chronological Structure

Narratives that simply tell what happened follow the chronological structure. Ten narratives were classified as chronological, representing 14% of the total collected. An example of this chronological structure is presented:

Fight

1.   A. Can you tell me about when you've had fights at school?

2.   C. this year?

3.   A. yeah

4.   C. I had a fight with' dis boy name Leo

5.   A. what happened?

6.   C. I beat 'im up!

7.   A. what did he say to you?

8.   C. He be all takin's junk in schoo'

9.   C. an' always think the, an' alway think da teacher gonna
     back it up an' stuff

10. C. an' then, an' then I be like, wait after schoo' after schoo'

11. C. an' then, he walks to it

12. C. an' den I jus' beat 'im up

13. A. you just beat him up?

14. C. yup

In the narrative, the narrator lists a series of events in response to the prompt administered by the investigator. In line 4, there is an orientation presented with little elaboration. For instance in line 6, he states the result: " I beat 'im up!". In line 7, the investigator asks for more information about the fight. Lines 8-12 are chronological statements. The narrative does not have an evaluation of the event. The complicating action had to be inferred by the listener. This narrative is a list of events of a fight by two boys and was coded as chronological.

Leapfrogging Structure

In this structure, children jump from event to event unsystematically. The children between ages 7 and 10 produced this type of structure. There were nine narratives classified as leapfrogging, representing 13% of the narratives collected. Five were at the 8-year-old level. Three of the narratives produced in this age range were by subject, while the remaining four narratives were by four different children. An example of leapfrogging structure is presented:

Scared

1.   C. When when when it's dark in my room on Halloween

2.   C. 'cause my my cousin

3.   C. I was sleepin'

4.   C. My cousin he he cut all da lights off

5.   C. I wasn' asleep

6.   C. but my cousin he cut all da lights off

7.   C. an' I started to scream

8.   C. an' my cousin he kep' laughin'

9.   C. an' my mother she tol' my cousin's mother

10.   C. an' my cousin got in trouble

11.   C. an' den another time when we went trick or treatin' on Halloween night

12.   C. I got a big bag o' candy

13.   C. an' den my cousin he had he was like um one o' my cousins was ninja

14.   C. an' he had dis sword dis fake sword

15.   C. an' my other cousin he was um Freddy Krueger and he had dese claws

16.   C. an' I was scared 'cause he was I was scared

17.   C. an' las' night I had dream dat me

18.   C. me an' you know Tierra?

19.   C. me an' Tierra, she came over my house

20.   C. me an' Tierra was playin' outside in da dark in da middle o' da night

21.   C. an' an' Freddy Krueger came and kep' chasin' us

22.   C. an' all my cousin we kep' runnin' da store

23.   C. I had a dream 'bout dat

In this narrative, the narrator does not follow a linear structure of one event. Instead she talks about three events that are thematically related to the prompt. Lines 1-3 are an orientation of the first event. The time was Halloween, the place was a room. The characters were the narrator and her cousin. The time was at night. The complicating action begins in line 4 and ends in line 7. The result is presented in line 10. Line 11 begins the next event about trick-or- treating on Halloween. The orientation is in lines 11- 15. In line 16, there is a reaction that she got scared.

The third event is a dream which begins in line 17. The orientation is in lines 17 - 20. The characters in the event are the narrator and Tierra. The time was at night and the place was outside. The complicating action begins in line 21 and ends in line 22. There is no result, and this event would be considered ending at the high point.

Ending-at-the -Highpoint Structure

In the ending-at-the-highpoint structure, the narrator provides successive complicating action until the highpoint is reached. Although the highpoint is dwelled upon, there is no result. Four narratives were coded as ending-at- the-highpoint, representing 6% of narratives collected. An example of ending-at-the-highpoint is presented from the Grandma/trouble prompt.

Grandma/trouble

1. A. What kind of stuff what happen?
2. C. um when when my motha she she was sleepin'
3. C. An' my baby brotha he's so bad
4. C. He keep um goin' like you know he
5. C. An' take my motha she she saves bottles like five cents bottles
6. C. My baby brotha always would go in da kitchen
7. C. She has a sink an' a cabinet on da bottom
8. C. My little brotha always goes in da cabinet take all da bottles out an' like
9. C. An' yesterday he broke one
10. A. He broke it and what happened?
11. C. My my my big my big brother five years ol' an' he blamed it on me

In this narrative, the orientation occurs in lines 2 and 3. The characters in the narrative are the narrator, mother and baby brother and the time reference is when the mother was sleeping. The complicating action begins on line 4 and ends on line 9 (the brother broke a bottle). In line 10 the investigator asks for more information. The narrator elaborates on the complicating action but does not give a result of the baby brother's behavior. It is not clear if the narrator is talking about one or two brothers. Earlier in the text, lines 3, 6, and 8, the narrator states little or baby brother, while in line 11 big brother is stated.

Impoverished Structure

Within the impoverished structure, narratives may consist of too few sentences to be analyzed. Only one narrative was coded as being impoverished, thus representing 1% of the narratives collected. An example of the impoverished structure using the funny prompt is presented:

Summary of Evaluative Results

The seven evaluative structures were analyzed for frequency across groups. Across all age groups, the children produced more classic structures. Groups 1 and 2 performed similarly while there was an increase in classic production with Group 3. The results suggested a developmental trend for structures with the exception of leapfrogging. No developmental trend existed within narrative structures across all three groups. There was a steady increase in production from Group 1 to Group 2 and a decrease thereafter. This small sample within groups prevented statistical treatment to assess the magnitude of differences across groups. The results of this study suggest that some African American children produce sophisticated narratives. The results of this analysis reveal that some African American children overwhelmingly produce narratives that are "topic centered" as described by the literature (Michaels, 1981). Children produced 66% of their narratives in the classic pattern as described through evaluative analysis.

The children in this study used the classic pattern, a total of 66%, most frequently, followed by the chronological and leapfrogging patterns; they used the ending-at-the-highpoint and impoverished patterns less frequently. Nine narratives classified as leapfrogging, representing 13% of narratives collected. The leapfrogging pattern is similar to the topic associating pattern that Michaels (1981) described. Six percent of the narratives in this study were coded as ending-at-the-highpoint. Within the present study the narrative that was coded as being impoverished was produced by an 8-year-old, representing 1% of the total narratives analyzed. Overall, the participants in this study produced narratives that were complex and sophisticated. The next chapter examines narratives using episodic analysis.

5
Episodic Narratives

All of the narratives produced by children were analyzed using episodic analysis. Seven structural patterns were analyzed: the descriptive pattern, the action sequence, the reactive sequence, the abbreviated pattern, and the complete, complex, and interactive episodes. The results are presented on two levels: overall production of structures and patterns within groups.

Overall Production of Structures

A total of 71 structures were produced. Each child produced a minimum of three structures, but some children produced more. In order of prevalence, from most prevalent to least prevalent, these structures can be classified as: complex, complete, reactive, interactive, and the action sequence pattern. Each of these episodic structures is discussed.

Complex Episodes

In complex episodes there are four types of patterns. The first two types of complex episodes can have one structure functioning as a single unit in a higher unit. This structure that functions as a single unit could be a reactive sequence or a complete episode. The third and fourth structures within this category involved some kind of complication in the pursuit of the goal. In the third type of structure a plan application may be repeated if the first attempt to reach the goal is not successful. In the fourth structure, not only is the plan repeated but there may also be an embedded episode. In the present study, 28 narratives (39%) were coded as being complex. An example of type three follows:

Sick

1.   A. How about a time when you were sick?
2.   C. I went to the doctors
3.   C. An' my mom, she had to see if I had asthma
4.   C. An' I had to go to the um store to get my medicine
5.   C. An' um they didn't have it
6.   C. An' I had to wait for 'em them to make it
7.   C. An' um my mom she wen' back again
8.   C. An' so she kep't on goin'g back an' back an' finally it was done making it
9.   C. An' I xx, when I got in the car an' she got it

10.   C. I had to drink some, i's nasty The narrator orients her
          listener (2) to the setting and the participants in the event.

The listener can infer that an adult has taken the child to the doctor's office. In line 3, the narrator confirms who has taken her to the doctor and gives the reason why the trip was necessary. In line 4, it may be inferred that some illness related to asthma was indicated. The goal of getting the medication was attempted a few times. Finally, in line 9, the goal was achieved.

Complete Episodes

With complete episodes there is a goal which requires planning on the part of the child. In this structure, children produced a minimum of two constituents from the following four possible constituents: the event, the motivating state, the attempt, and the consequence. There were a total of 25 complete episodes, representing 35% of narratives collected. An example of complete episode is below:

1.   A. Tell me one time and tell me what happened

2.   C. My sister spill her juice 'cause we were about to go over
         grandma's house and get wet in da pool

3.   C. las' summer ( )

4.   C. and so I didn' know my mother tol' me ta help her

5.   C. An' den she yelled at me

6.   C. an' den (child's name) didn't hafta clean it up

7.   C. I had to clean up the whole thing

In this narrative the goal is for the juice to be cleaned up by the sister. The setting appears to be at home and the time is the summer. The characters in the narrative are the narrator, sister and mother. The event is presented in line 1 (the juice is spilled). Lines 4 and 5 are a reaction from the narrator being scolded by her mother. Lines 6 and 7 are the consequence of the juice event. The narrator, instead of the sister, had to clean up the juice.

Reactive Sequences

A reactive sequence is comprised of a series of statements that may or may not be causally related to each other. Children produced nine reactive sequences, representing 13% of narratives collected. An example of reactive sequence is below:

1.   A. You never had a hard time . . . in school?

2.   C. Yeah a hard time wit my work in school

3.   C. A hard time when I had in school right? just work right?

4.   A. un huh

5. C. we never ( )

6. C. they gave us cursive, all dat stuff

7. C. we not suppose to get cursive yet

7. A. Why not?

8. C. I don't know

9. C. The substitute gave it to us

10. C. We have a substitute all week again because my teacher was in a car accident

11. A. Oh really

12. C. I'm tellin everybody dat now

13. A. you tellin' everybody what, that your teacher was in a car accident

14. C. yeah, car accident

15. A. Oh, ok

16. A. so what happened with the substitute

17. C. She givin us cursive

18. C. like we can' even do cursive

19. C. an she givin' befo' our teacher

20. C. an' we don' even do cursive

The prompt for this narrative was "tell me a time when you had a hard time." In this narrative there appears to be two events that are linked together by the topic hard time. One event leads to another event. The first event begins in lines 2 and 3. The setting is school. The characters are the substitute teacher, the class and the narrator. There is no goal or planning evident in this event. The narrator complains in lines 6 and 7 about being told that the class had to write in cursive instead of print. She ends this event in line 9.

In line 10 she begins another event about a substitute teacher but the focus is on why the teacher is absent from school. Her teacher was in a car accident (lines 10, 14). The setting is the school and the same characters are present. In line 16 the investigator tries to redirect the child to talk about the substitute. In lines 17-19, the consequence of writing in cursive is presented. In lines 20 she reacts to being told to write in cursive.

Interactive Episodes

In this category, there were two types of interactive episodes. One type of episode involves two or more people who have goals that influence each other. The second type in this category involves two people who respond to each other. There is no evidence of planning, and a typical discourse involves "he said, she said." With respect to this pattern, 8% of narratives were coded as interactive. An example of an interactive episode follows:

1.   A. Can you tell me a time when you got real mad at somebody?

2.   C. Today in gym

3.   A. What happened?

4.   C. I was talkin' to my frien'

5.   C. An' she an' da other girl said "be quiet"

6.   C. An' she was yellin

7.   C. An' den she sa.., an' she said "yes you do"

8.   C. An' I I already talked about her

9.   C. An' I was like, because she said dat I was talkin' ah

10.   C. An' my frien' was wit' me

11.   C. She isn' my frien' no more

12.   C. She told she told da girl gonna run over an' see what's goin' on

13.   C. An' she said I wouldn' tell

14.   C. An' I di'n't trust her

15.   C. Also, I di'n't tell her nothin' about it

16.   C. An' den Naquia said den dis girl girl another girl came over an' wen' over and told to

17.   C. I said Toya uh don't talk loud cause Latoya gonna be um gonna be listenin' what we say say about Kayla

18.   C. An' we wasn' even sayin' nothin' about her

19.   C. And um, dey thought we was talkin' about her

Two episodes appear in this narrative. In the first, the setting is in the gym and the characters are the narrator and two girls. The event begins in line 4, with the narrator speaking with her friend. In lines 5-9 another girl interrupts the conversation. The narrator and the other girl begin a dialogue of accusations concerning talking about the other. In lines 10 and 11, there is a consequence and a reaction to the dialogue by the narrator. The episode is incomplete, however, because there is no goal or planning taking place.

Line 12 begins another episode. The event is the narrator's ex-friend talking behind her back. The goal of the event is to see if someone is talking behind another person's back. The rest of the episode is a back -and -forth conversation about who is talking to and about whom. There is no planning or consequence in this episode.

This type of narrative has been described by Goodwin (1990) as <u>he said/she said</u> narrative. Goodwin defines this type of discourse as "an initial gossip stage in which the current defendant is alleged to have talked about her accuser in her absence. An intermediate stage in which the girl who was talked about learns about the offense committed against her from a third party and the third descriptor is the confrontation itself " (p. 190).

Action sequences

The action sequence is described by Peterson and McCabe (1983) as a narrative that focuses on the actions of the protagonist. This pattern was produced once by an 8-year-old subject. An example of this structure, using the funny prompt, is given.

Funny

    1.   A. Has there been a time when something funny happened?

    2.   C. In school, I had um, had ketchup when I splatted it in my dis boy dat sat next

    3.   C. I spatted it in his face an' on his desk an' on my face too

In this type of narrative the focused on behavior. The setting is in school and the characters are the narrator and a boy. The narrator repeats the statement of spitting ketchup on the boy.

Patterns Within Groups

The total number of narrative structures produced by the children in each age group is shown in Table 5.1.

Complex Episodes. All children across the age groups produced over 25% of their narratives in the complex category. Groups 1 and 2 had 43%, while Group 3 had 32% of their narratives in this category.

Complete Episodes. Group 1 produced 48% of narratives coded as being complete. Group 2 produced five complete narratives, representing 22% of the total. Thirty six percent of the narratives in Group 3 were coded as being complete.

Reactive Sequences. The 6-year-old within Group 1 had no reactive sequences. Group 1 as a whole had 9% of their narratives coded as being reactive. For Group 2, 22% of the narratives coded were reactive. Group 3 had 8% of their narratives coded as reactive.

TABLE 5.1

Percentage of Episodic Structures Within Groups

| | Group | | | | | | | |
| | 1 | | 2 | | 3 | | Total | |
Structure	n	%	n	%	n	%	n	%
Complex	10	43	10	43	8	32	28	39
Complete	11	48	5	22	9	36	25	35
Reactive	2	9	5	22	2	8	9	13
Interactive	0	0	0	0	4	16	4	6
Interactive Reactive	0	0	2	9	2	8	4	6
Action Sequence	0	0	1	4	0	0	1	1
Total	23	100	23	100	25	100	71	100

Interactive Episodes. Group 2 produced 9% of their narratives in the interactive category. Group 3 produced 22% in this category.

Patterns Within Groups. All children across all ages produced over 25% of their narratives in the complex category. Groups 1 and 2 had 43% of their narratives fit into this category, and Group 3 had 32% of their narratives in this category. Group 1 produced 48% of their narratives coded as being complete. Group 2 produced 5 narratives, representing 22% of the total, while Peterson and McCabe's total number of narratives coded as complete was 51% of the narratives collected. Thirty- six percent of the narratives in Group 3 were coded as complete.

Children produced fewer complete structures but had a higher frequency of complex structures. This finding suggests that children are able to produce the most complex type of narratives.

Group 1 had 9% of their narratives coded as reactive, while in Group 2, 22% of the narratives coded were reactive. Group 3 had 8% of their narratives coded as reactive.

Group 2 produced 9% of their narratives in the interactive category, while Group 3 produced 22% in this category.

Summary of Episodic Analysis

To summarize, a total of 71 narratives were produced. Each participant produced a minimum of three narratives. In this study, 28 (39%) were coded as complex. There were a total 25 complete episodes, representing 35% of narratives collected. Participants produced 13% (9) reactive sequences, and 12 narratives were produced as interactive episodes. As far as the patterns within the groups, Groups 1 and 2 had 43%, and Group 3 had 32% of its narratives classified as complex. Group 1 produced 48% of narratives as complete episodes, while Group 2 produced 22%. Group 3 produced 36% of their narratives as complete. In the reactive sequence category, Group 1 produced 9%, Group 2 produced 22% and Group 3 had 8%. For the interactive category, Group 2 produced 9%, while Group 3 produced 24% in the category. Overall, the participants in this study produced 74% of their narratives as either complete or complex episodes. The next two chapters examine the same 71 narratives using thematic and sociolinguistic analyses.

6
Moral Centered Narratives

The recurring theme of a moral dilemma became evident when categorizing and sorting narratives through thematic analysis. The narratives were not examined to fit an a priori structure of what was missing from the narrative, as in evaluative and episodic analyses. This approach differs, then, from that presented in the previous chapters. There were 12 narratives categorized by the "moral" theme, produced by at least one third of the children. The moral centered type of narrative appeared to differ from the "evaluative" and "episodic" structures. In this structure the narrator embeds a lesson to be learned by the listener/audience. In the narrative by Loretta, a 10-year-old African American female, the narrator used a moral dilemma to transmit a message to the listener:

Loretta

1.	A.	Have you ever been a hero?
2.	C.	Yes I been a hero to my brother, my brother an' my friens.
3.	C.	Well, I was ridin' my bike down da street
4.	C.	And um an my friend who was goin real fast 'cause I was taggin' er
5.	C.	An I da thing and had a race to see who'd won
6.	C.	An I was an I an I was tweeny seconds cause I had I had big gear
7.	C.	An' I zoomin' an' she comin' slow
8.	C.	I woulda had forty seconds
9.	C.	I was countin' myself an she counts so she says tweeny seconds
10.	C.	An' I said your turn
11.	C.	I had a timer watch
12.	C.	An' she was racing down da street
13.	C.	An she run she was zoomin on da bike
14.	C.	She's use my bike
15.	C.	She didn' know how da gear
16.	C.	An' I said do you know how
17.	C.	An' she say she did 'cause she alway like to be you know it all
18.	C.	An' I said don' say you know if you don'

19.   C. She said I know

20.   C. An den a little girl was walkin' across da street an comin across da street

21.   C. An' she'd been runnin'

22.   C. She was goin' real fast

23.   C. An I an I said her name was Kim

24.   C. An' I said watch out watch out

25.   C. An she didn' hear me cause she had a walkman on

26.   C. An' um it was mine though 'cause I let all my friends use my stuff

27.   C. An I an I run as fas' as I could

28.   C. An I just in time before she was' close to her I pushed her aside

29.   C. An an den um an den she an den den um she an I pushed her aside

30.   C. An I moved aside so she wouldn't hit her

31.   C. An den den she said where was dat little girl at?

32.   C. An I said she came across da street an you almos' hit her

33..   C. An she got she da little girl up

34.   C. She said sorry

35.   C. An da las thing dat happened was she jus' threw my bike in da road an dat'ts how it broke

36.   C. Now I need another one

37.   C. I have a kickstand

38.   C. But she didn' put it down

39.   C. She jus threw it

40.   C. I said da bike

41.   C. I said da little girl was importan'

42.   C. But you didn't have throw it down

43.   C. An' I saved 'er

44.   C. You were gonna hit 'er

45.   C. And dats all

The narrative is structured around lines 15 through 19, which has the moral problem, the reason why the narrative is being told. In lines 3 through 9, the narrator sets the first scene of the story. The characters are introduced (lines 3 and 4). There is a change in line 10, which begins another scene within this narrative. In line 14, the narrator states "she's use my bike." This statement is right before the introduction of the moral problem, the crux of the story. Loretta uses this statement in line 14 to introduce the dilemma.

Loretta chose to use dialogue to embed her moral lesson and thus is teaching by example. Instead of saying directly to the listener it is important to be honest, the narrator shows through example what happens if you are not honest (lines 22, 24, 28, and 32). In line 15, Loretta uses the word "didn't" as an evaluative device (see Labov, 1972). In this line, Loretta is evaluating a type of knowledge that her friend should have if she is going to ride the bike knowing how to use gears to ride the bike. Although Loretta knew that her friend did not have the needed knowledge, and stated this in line 15, she gave her the options of either telling the truth or lying (line 16) by asking her, "Do you know how?" In line 17, there are two parts to the utterance: the answer by the friend, and the narrator's own thoughts. The friend chose to be dishonest with the narrator, and in the second part of the statement the narrator evaluates the friend's answer, claiming that the friend likes to be "you know it all." She uses the "always" to emphasize this point. In line 18, the narrator responds by telling the friend not to say she knows if she doesn't. Loretta is also challenging the friend to be honest because no one could possibly always know everything. In line 19, the friend responds with, "I know."

Loretta has given her friend two opportunities to answer honestly using the technique of piling and association. By examining the surface structure of this passage (lines 15 to 19), we see that each line has the word "know" in it. This might give the mistaken impression that the discussion concerned only knowledge or the lack of knowledge. But if we look at lines 15, 17 and 18, in which the narrator is talking, we see that the narrator is evaluating the situation. This signals to the listener that the situation is deeper than possessing knowledge or having a lack of knowledge.

In the last scene, lines 20 through 44, Loretta states the consequence of the moral problem. First a new character (the catalyst) is introduced into the story in line 20. In lines 20 and 24, the narrator uses repetition to add suspense to her story. In line 26, she digresses, talking about sharing possessions. The narrator evaluates her own moral behavior by stating, "I let all my friends use my stuff."

In lines 28 and 29 Loretta uses lexical parallelism and repetition ("I pushed her aside"). Also, in lines 35 and 39, there is a repetition of "she jus' threw it," indicating lexical parallelisms. Lexical parallelism is used as an evaluative device for emphasis. In this narrative, the narrator is evaluating the moral behavior of her friend.

At the beginning of line 35, Loretta informs the listener that the narrative is coming to an end. Lines 35 through 39 are an evaluation of the moral problem of lines 15 to 19. In lines 40 and 41, lexical parallelism is again used. In line 42, Loretta states directly how she feels about how her friend behaved with her property. In lines 43 and 44, she ends the narrative but leaves it in the past tense, giving the narrative a dramatic ending. The narrator successfully builds up to a suspense. In line 45, the narrative ends with a coda.

To summarize, Loretta's narrative is structured around a moral dilemma, that of honesty. She strengthens her narrative with stylistic characteristics, using lexical parallelism, piling, and repetition to build suspense. She associates honesty/lying with consequences, and communicates her intent. She evaluates both her own and her friend's behavior. All these are characteristics mentioned by Okpewho in African oral storytelling traditions.

Terri, an 8- year old female, provides another example of a moral narrative:

1.   A. Can you tell me a time you were really angry?
2.   C. OK I got mad 'cause my brother he
3.   C. I was angry 'cause my brother, brothers they always mess up my room so much
4.   C. an' I had to get
5.   C. my mom she yells at me when when somethin' happens in the house
6.   C. see my big brothers my seventeen little my seventeen he he had to he had to clean up behind me when I was little child
7.   C. das what he told me
8.   C. den when he moved out I had clean little brothers
9.   C. an' I said "I'm gittin' sick o' dis
10.   C. I don' wanna do dis no more
11.   C. dey gonna clean up for dey own self
12.   C. I had to clean all up when dey make a mess
13.   C. den I said "next time you make a mess you eat on de floor wit' de paper
14.   C. but they make they only little childrens so dey little children have to make a mess
15.   C. when I was little I had to make a mess
16.   C. so dey didn' eat on de floor dough
17.   C. I had had to clean after dem

Lines 2 through 7 reflect Scene 1 of the narrative. Terri introduces the problem in lines 2 and 3. Terri brings it to the listener's attention that her brother is an important character in the narrative. She then sets the stage for the moral dilemma in line 5. This line represents the backbone of the narrative and sets up how the rest of the narrative will be interpreted. From this line we know that the narrator must take responsibility for events in the home. In lines 6 and 7, she indicates how responsibility has been handled in her family. She also uses the piling of information in line 6 to describe her older brother. In the second scene, which begins in line 8, there is a passing down of responsibility. In lines 11, 14, and 15 the narrator makes moral statements about her dilemma. This narrative appears to represent an inner dilemma for Terri. She is in the process of trying to decide the right action to perform in what appears to be a no-win situation for herself. If she doesn't clean up after her brothers she will get in trouble. She also wants to pass on the responsibility but realizes that she cannot until she moves out.

In this example, Terri talks about a time when she was angry. She talked about how she had to clean up after her brothers (lines 9, 10, 11, and 12). In line 13, the narrator states that the next time her brother makes a mess the consequence will be that they will have to eat on the floor. In lines 12, 13, 14 , 15 and 17, Terri uses repetition of the phrases "had to clean" and "make a mess"—which are opposites —to emphasize the moral dilemma involved with taking care of her siblings. In line 14, the narrator imparts on the listener her philosophy about the behavior of the young. In line 9, the narrator states she is frustrated by cleaning after her brother. In line 11, she implies that it is time for them to be responsible for their mess. In line 13, the narrator implies that if her brother is not responsible there will be a consequence. Throughout this passage Terri uses the negative evaluation device. She uses negative statements in lines 10 and 16, and in lines 12, 14, 15, and 17, she uses compulsive words to evaluate the situation. Earlier, the narrator justifies cleaning up after her younger brother because her older brother had to do the same for her. In line 14, she decides that it is okay for children to be messy. She is implying that children do not have self-control or the knowledge that they have to clean up after themselves. The narrator states in line 15 that when she was little she also made a mess. At the time of the data collection, the narrator was 8 years old. She lets us know that the age range for her brothers is under 8 years old. She ends this passage with "I had to clean after dem." It may be that the narrator did not have a choice in the matter. The responsibility has been passed down in her family.

This is not a straight forward narrative like Loretta's but has the charateristic of morality that researchers (Okpewho, 1992; Levine, 1977) have discussed. Thus,

Terri's narrative is structured around the moral dilemma presented in line 5. The narrator uses different lexical strategies, repetition, piling and association to continually evaluate the dilemma put forth earlier in the text.

The next narrative is by Dora, a 9-year-old African American female. The prompt was "Tell me a time when you were sick":

1.   A. ever been sick?

2.   C. yeah, a time when I was sick. . .

3.   C. I can tell a time when my friend been sick

4.   C. an' she din' come ta school

5.   C. an' an' she had ta come ta school

6.   C. an' she missed all of her work

7.   C. she even missed all of her work

8.   C. she even missed da art work

9.   C. she even missed da art project

10.   C. an' she was an' she was mad because she was jus' fakin...

11.   C. because she said it

12.   A. So she's mad because what did she miss

13.   C. she missed two art projects, um her (unintelligible utterance) where you have when another class came an' you read an' dey had da read it

14.   C. an' dere was (unintelligible utterance) where she missed lots o' other things, but I forgot dem

15.   C. an' she was real mad

16.   C. an' I said dat was your fault

17.   C. you shouda never been sick

The narrative is structured around lines 10 and 11, which contain the moral problem, the reason why the narrative is being told. In line 1, a question is put on the floor by the investigator. In line 2 Dora answers the question. In line 3, she introduces the main character (my frien') and the topic (being sick). In line 4, the narrator provides the results of her friend being sick. Lines 3 and 4 together serve as an abstract for the narrative. From these two lines the audience knows that the story will be about a young person not going to school because she is sick. In lines 6 through 9, the narrator uses repetition and the piling of information. In line 6, the narrator states that the main character missed her work. In line 7, Dora emphasizes this statement by repeating it. For more emphasis, she uses the 'even' before the repetition of the statement. She continues the use of 'even' in lines 7, 8, and 9. In lines 12 through 14, the narrator piles on more detail about how the main character missed school. From all of her statements it appears that art work is an important event for these young people. Lines 10 and 11 serve as the crux of the narrative. Here, the narrator states the moral dilemma: The main character faked being sick in order to miss school. In lines 15, 16 and 17, the narrator uses dialogue to examine and judge morality. The narrator uses inferences in lines 16 and 17 to tell the listener about the main character. The narrator recounts the missed reading and other things that she forgot. However, the art projects are emphasized throughout the narrative (lines 8, 9 and 13), and that faking illness will lead to negative consequences.

To summarize, Dora's narrative is structured around a moral dilemma. This strategy is similar to Loretta's narrative when her moral dilemma is the crux of the narrative. Similar to Loretta's narrative strategic style, Dora's uses lexical parallelism, piling, and repetition throughout the narrative which are the characteristics discussed by Okpewho (1992).

The next narrative is by Shaka, a 10-year-old African American male. The prompt was "Tell me a time you were angry."

1.   A. Oh, can you tell me about a time (you were angry)?

2.   C. when, dey I got real mad because my brother always got his way

3.   C. an' an' my mother's roo- I got mad

4.   C. an' I punched her window an' it broke

5.   C. an' so den when she got home

6.   C. an' so den when got home

7.   C. I told 'er that I tripped an' fell an' hit it

8.   C. but den like the nex' month I told er the truth

9.   A. and so what did she say?

10.   C. she said oh so you lied to me an' I said yep

11.   C. she din' do nothin'

Shaka presents the complicating action in line 4 (an' I punched her window an' it broke). In lines 2 and 3, Shaka introduces the characters—the narrator, the brother and the mother—are introduced. The narrator informs the audience early in the narrative why he is angry. It appears to be a sibling conflict, with his brother seemingly getting his way with their mother. The narrator uses lexical parallelism and repetition in lines 5 and 6. In line 7, the moral dilemma is presented;

in addition, the narrator reports what he told his mother about the broken window. The narrator does not tell the truth (that he broke the window). In line 8, the narrator reports to the audience that he told the truth to his mother the next month. In line 9, the investigator asks a question. Shaka responds in lines 10 and 11, and ends both the interaction and the narrative.

The narrator centers the narrative on line 7, the moral dilemma. At first the narrative appears to be about anger; however, as Shaka continues the narrative he places the issue of telling the truth on the floor. This shifts the narrative from a highpoint structure to a moral structure. Shaka solves his dilemma by stating that he told his mother the truth about the broken window a month later.

In the next narrative , Christine, an 8-year-old girl, uses a moral dilemma to transmit a message to the listener:

1.   A. Do you know anybody who had to get stitched?

2.   C. mm a boy in my secon' grade class name Evan he he was running an uh at schoo'

3.   C. an' da lady tol' him not to be runnin'

4.   C. He didn' listen to her

5.   C. He didn' listen to her

6.   C. An he fell straight on 'cause it was in da winter

7.   C. An he fell straight on da footsteps where you step at

8.   C. an' it's like a curve thing

9.   C. an' dere was ice on it

10.   C. an' he fell

11.   C. an an den da nex' day he didn' come to school

12.   C. So so when he didn' come to school he had ta um he had da get stitches

13.   C. An den a few weeks later he came in

14.   C. An' he go da stitches

15.   C. an' it was nasty

16.   C. dey was nasty

17.   C. dey was black

This narrative is structured around a moral problem (line 5). The first scene opens with the setting, which includes the location and the characters. In line 2, Christine introduces the main character, Evan. She then states that he was running at school. With this introduction, the narrator sets up the framework that there is a certain behavior that one practices in a school setting. In line 3, the narrator states that Evan was told not to run. Although Christine does not tell us the status of the person who tells Evan not to run, she does say "da lady," which implies that Evan, who is in the second grade, should be listening to the lady, who is an adult. Lines 2 and 3 are in contrast to each other (line 2: mm a boy in my secon' grade class name Evan he was running an uh school / line 3: an da lady tol' him not to be runnin).

In line 2, we have a child named Evan who was running. In line 3, we have "da lady tol' him not to be runnin." The narrator is using negative words to evaluate the situation. In lines 4 and 5 using repetition, the narrator tells us that Evan continued running. In line 5, she evaluates the behavior in line 4, using negation. Lines 2 and 4 state the behavior, while lines 3 and 5 evaluate the behavior. Christine does not overtly state the moral of the narrative, but she infers that Evan should follow rules and listen to and respect adults. In line 6, the result is that Evan fell down, implying that if Evan had followed the rules and listened to the adult, he would not have fallen down. Christine uses repetition and piling of information to highlight information in the narrative. In lines 2 and 3 , running was repeated two times. In lines 6, 7, and 10, the narrator repeats "he fell" three times. In lines 7, 8, 9 and in lines 15, 16,and 17, information was emphasized using the narrative technique of piling information. Finally, in lines 11 and 12, the sentence, "he didn't come to school" was repeated. In this narrative, Christine uses the moral centered structure, illustrating that children should listen to their elders. In addition, she uses stylistic techniques such as repetition, parallelism and piling to emphasize this point.

In this study, 12 narratives out of 71 were coded as moral centered. This category was explored by Champion (1995), who defined this structure as the embedding of a moral lesson within a narrative. In this type of narrative the narrator structures the narrative around a moral theme. Trickster tales from West Africa and the Caribbean often have moral lessons embedded in the story. Therefore, the telling of the story takes on more significance because in it, the narrator passes down values and morals that one is expected to achieve or emulate. In the same vein, the children in this study realize that values and morals are important for their well-being.

In the moral centered narrative a moral dilemma forms the base of the structure. The use of a dilemma as an element is similar to the evaluative and episodic structures. However, in the evaluative or episodic structures, morality may not be at the base of the narrative. This is different from Loretta's narrative in which the theme of honesty is played out in this dilemma. Loretta chose to focus her narrative on lines 15 through 19 because she was interested in evaluating the values and the morals of her friend. In the beginning, the listener assumes that the narrative is going to be about the narrator as 'hero.' It appeared up to line 13 that the narrative was following the structure of episodic analysis. However, in the next couple of lines, there is a shift in the structure of the narrative. The narrator relates a conversation between herself and the friend, thereby breaking the linear structure of time. The conversation the narrator had with her friend occurred in the past. If we examine this structure using culture as a bridge, one way to interpret the conversation in the narrative is the use of an evaluation technique (Labov, 1972) of stepping out of the narrative to evaluate why the story is being told. Another way to interpret the narrative is that the narrator has shifted the structure of the narrative. The narrator has changed the structure from an episodic or evaluative narrative to telling a moral centered narrative. Thus the goal of the narrative is the moral content and not the dilemma.

It is significant that the conversation took place in the past. The time shift can signify a circular pattern of time, which is consistent with at least one concept of time in West Africa. Simultaneously, the narrative is both in the present and in the past. This time shift produces a narrative that is in a circular pattern instead of a linear pattern. This concept is important in the African and African American communities. Ani (1994) states that past, present and future represents a multidimensional view of time. If we accept that time does not have to be linear then the past, the present and the future can exist in any order in a narrative and still be coherent to the listener. The narrator is an integral element of the narrative and is not alienated from it. The characters in the narrative are significant in that they enable the narrator to explore the importance of both her community and her relationships. She is an active participant in the narrative. The goal of the narrative is to relate a point about honesty. The second point is to explore the importance of community. The narrator begins by talking about her brothers and then moves on to a discussion about her friends. The narrative is multidimensional because it is about a community of people. At the same time, it focuses on teaching a moral lesson.

The moral centered structure appears to have links to African American culture and possibly to West African culture (see Michaels, 1981; Michaels & Foster, 1985; Michaels & Collins, 1984, Heath; 1983). Researchers who have studied narrative production in West Africa have pointed out that some narratives are centered on teaching children values and morals (Okpewho, 1992; Levine, 1977). Researchers reported similar findings among African Americans in the United States (Smitherman, 1977; Brewer, 1972; Gates, 1989).

7

Performative Narratives

Eight narratives produced by children in this study were coded as being "performative," representing 11% of the total narratives. The performance structure also emerges from the data as a result of the observation that the eight narratives appeared to have similarities. The first similarity is the "telling" or "performance" of the narrative that forms the body of the narrative. Further analysis, using an interactional sociolinguistic perspective, revealed that narratives in this structure emphasized interaction between the audience and the narrator. In addition, the use of this perspective indicated a heavy use of paralinguistic strategies, including the manipulation of tempo, intonation contours, rhythm, pause, vowel elongation, and stress. Other strategies included the use word and <u>sound repetitions</u> <u>information piling</u> and <u>nonverbal gestures</u>.

For these performance narratives, a key chart is presented:

Key

^	pitch in intonation is higher
!	pitch in intonation is lower
( )	unintelligible word
. . .	long speech pause
. .	speech pause
:	vowel elongation

The first narrative is by Terri, an 8-year-old African American female. The prompt for the narrative was : "I used to play with my friend Audrey when I was younger. One day we were playing outside and we were being chased by some boys on the block. We ran inside my apartment. My little baby brother was sleeping. When we ran in we woke him up and he started crying. My aunt came into the room and said , 'You woke him up, you put him back to sleep.' Did anything like that ever happen to you or someone you know?"

Terri

```
      H——— L H ^H H———^H————-H
1.    you know how..! parents smoke cigarettes

2.    adult: un huh

      H———-^H H——!H L ^H———L
3.    rosalind .. ! she was only.. 15 or 14
```

```
      H——————‚ !H——————!H L —L H———-H
```
4.   she w-she sneaks in my grandmothers room.. !get a cigarette

```
      H————— L
```
5.   ^then she wake us up

```
      H————L!H————!H—-L !HH
```
6.   !and she make my cousin do a cigarette

```
      H———H—H
```
7.   !but my cousin don't

acc

```
      H L—H————H
```
8.   she he went to go tell my grandmother

acc

```
      H !H !HL
```
9.   !and sometimes he gets up

```
      H
```
0.   and sometimes she gets up

```
      L ! H L H L
```
11.   and watch soap operas e:arly at nighttime

```
      H L        H      L
```
12.   !and then wake us up .. to watch soap operas

13.   un huh

```
      H L — H———— H—-H
```
14.   what my grandmother taped

```
      L H ——— H— ^H———H
```
15.   cause my grandmother .. ^use to tape .. soap operas

16.   adult un huh

```
      ———L H————-H
```
17.   but when she find out

```
      H————H H-H
```
18.   !Rosalind been going in there with the tape

```
      LH—————‚ H* H———
```
19.   early in the morning watching the soap operas

20.   un huh

```
         ── L─────────H─────H
21.   ^cause rosalind like soap operas
```

22.   adult un huh

```
      L H── L H L H─────────────H
23.   !and she don't tape soap operas no more
```

```
      ──────── HH
24.   !but if she do
```

```
      H──────────HLH
25.   she puts them up somewhere
```

26.   oh ok

```
      H !H L H──
27.   and and one time .. Rosalind went in this room
```

```
      L+H────        HL H──H
28.   my grandfather .. he had some tapes
```

29.   un huh

```
      LH !H L
30.   ^and she went in there an watched it
```

```
      H L+ H !HL
31.   !an it was a ba:d tape
```

32.   adult: it was bad tape

33.   child yep

34.   adult un huh what was on the tape (child comes and
      whispers something to me)

35.   adult: oh

```
      LH────L──── H !H L
36.   an she got in bi:g trouble
```

37.   adult : oh she got in big trouble

```
      H──H
38.   child yep ( ) leave home (unintelligible)
```

39.   un huh

```
      HLH H─────────H─────H──H
40.   and .. then she had to go somewhere else
```

H——————— L————LH——————————L^H L
41.   ^cause my grandmother .. couldn't put up wif her n:o more

42.   adult: she couldn't put up wif her

43.   oh ok

L H L H ^H L HH L H+H
44.   but now shes grown .. shes fast .. !and shes fresh

HH H H————H
45.   ^she cuss ..^ she wear lipstick

H L H————————H
46.   ^she smokes cigarettes

L H HH
47.   ^tha:s bad

H——————————, ^H L L H——————————,H——————————H
48.   you know what .. you have .. if you smoke cigarettes

H L !H L+H !H
49.   you have black lungs

50.   adult: that's right

H H!H———— H
51.   !you can die like that

H H L————,
52.   you can get cancer and stuff

H H H H ————L H L
53.   !my mom teach me she told me not to smoke cigarettes

H——————— L——————————
54.   and i never smoke cigarettes

55.   ( ) cause cigarettes can make you die

56.   and that cigarette caffeine

H L H————H
57.   it got got drug in it

H !H H H H
58.   ^and my mom..! shes tryin to quit smoking

LH——————————, L H—————————————— H
59.   ^so .. you know what ^if you go around somebody

H H ^H——— H !H L H H ^H—H
60. if my mom !my teacher told me he says Mr. Skol he use to come

61. un huh

H H L   L H—-H
62. use to come um to our school

63. un huh

L H !H L H L L H
64. !an he said that .. ^ "if you around ^ some people thats

!H L H !H L
smoking ! dont be around them"

L H—-H!H———-H—-H
65. like .. ^go to another room

66. un huh

H———-, H—- H H—-H—————-H——H
67. !sometimes when mommy she smokes in her room

L H————H
!or in the living room

H————————H———H
68. ^an when she smokes in the living room I go in her room

69. I close the door

L H H H—-H
70. so ^if you be around them

71. un huh

———-L H !H !H—-H
72. and if you be around a smoker

H H L H————-H
73. an if you start breathing stuff

H !H————H—H
74. an the smoke will go in your nose

L H————L—
75. and go to your lungs

H H HL
76. then start turning really black probably (sucks teeth)

77. ok

There are five segments in Terri's narrative: lines 1 to 8, lines 9 to 26, lines 27 to 47, lines 48 to 58, and lines 59 to 77. All of the segments are connected to the theme, "smoking is bad for you." The shift of segments is marked by paralinguistic strategies. The discussion that follows focuses on how Terri shifted to each of the segments in her narrative. The first segment begins in line 1. Terri opened with a question. .She raised intonation and pitch on the words know, parents, and cigarettes. The rise at the end of each utterance signaled that there was more coming. In line 2, the adult responded by agreeing and requesting information from the narrator.

The shift to segment two begins in line 7 and finishes in line 8. In both of these lines the tempo was accelerated. The intonation was raised at the end of both utterances, signaling more to come. In the previous statements there was no introduction of tempo with a rise of intonation on the last word. The combination of tempo, intonation, and lexical items signaled that a new subtopic, beginning in line 9, was being introduced.

In segment three, which begins in lines 27 and 28, there were statements that used pauses, rhythm, intonation, and pitch to inform the listener that a new subtopic had started. Terri used the repetition of the word "and" to claim the floor again and to indicate the new subtopic. In both statements Terri used a high pitch and a rise in intonation at the end of the utterance. This rise in intonation at the end may have served to inform the listener that this subtopic was about tapes, but was different from the soap opera tapes talked about earlier. The new subtopic of tapes was about tapes that the grandfather had watched. In line 28, the narrator was asking the listener if she wanted to hear more. In lines 29, the listener/audience responds that different information was being presented. This response also let the narrator know that it was all right to start and continue with another subtopic.

In line 48, the narrator initiated a new subtopic with a question in which she used a high intonation with the question. This use of a high intonation was the same as in lines 1 and 4, which may indicate that the narrator was linking line 48 to line 1.

In the last segment, initiated in line 57, the narrator increased her volume; in addition, the pattern of ending with high intonation started again, along with the rhythm pattern. The increase in volume may have been used as a shift, one that began with line 57 and ended with line 58, a statement that ends on a high tone. In line 59, the shift was complete and had the same ending intonational pattern that was seen in line 48.

In each of the five segments the narrator produced a scene or unit with the theme of "smoking is bad for you" while tying the segments together. In the first segment, the narrator introduces the topic in line 1. In line 3, the main character is introduced. In lines 4, 5, and 6, the narrator presents the event of smoking cigarettes without permission. The result of the event is presented in lines 7 and 8 in which the cousin tells the grandmother about Rosalind's behavior.

In the next segment, lines 9 and 10 introduce the characters and the setting. From the previous segment we can infer that this segment is about Rosalind and the cousin. In lines 11 through 15, the event is presented. The children are watching taped soap operas without permission in the middle of the night. In lines 17, 18 and 19, the children are caught by the grandmother. The grandmother changes her behavior ("don't tape soap operas no more") but does not appear to be consistent ("but if she do") because the narrator states that the grandmother stores the tapes out of reach from the children.

In the third segment, both the setting (room), and the character (Rosalind), are presented in line 27. In lines 28 and 29, the narrator presents the event of Rosalind watching videotapes. In lines 31 and 36, the narrator evaluates the event. The result (in line 40) is that Rosalind is no longer living with her grandparents. In the rest of the segment the narrator continues to evaluate the event and Rosalind's behavior. The narrator correlates Rosalind's bad behavior to smoking cigarettes. She ends the segment by evaluating the implications of smoking cigarettes.

In the next segment (lines 48 to 58) the narrator continues the topic of smoking cigarettes with a different focus. The listener is told what will happen if she smokes cigarettes. First, she will have black lungs with the result of death. In addition, she could get cancer. The narrator ends the segment by reminding the listener that there are drugs in cigarettes.

In the last segment the narrator begins with a warning (lines 59 through 65) to keep away from smokers. In lines 67 to 69, the narrator gives an example from her life on how the listener can get away from the smoker. Finally, the narrator ends with a warning (lines 70 to 76) of what will happen if the listener breathes secondhand smoke.

Terri successfully uses performance aspects in her narrative. First, in Terri's narrative there is consistent interaction between the audience and the narrator. Within the 77 lines, the audience responds to the narrator 19 times. This interaction moves the narrative forward to its conclusion. Second, Terri utilizes stylistic features such as repetition (e.g., lines 9, 10, 44, 45, 46) and vowel elongation (e.g., lines 11, 31, and 36) to add drama to the production of the narrative.

The next narrative is by Rasheed, a 9-year-old African American male. The prompt was as follows: "Tell me a time when you were a hero."

1.   A. Can you tell me a time when you were a hero? Have you ever been a hero?

2.   C. yes my sister wen' up in da five feet an

3.   A. Up in the what?

4.   C. in da five feet 'cause she couldn' swim

5.   C. an' couldn' swim neither

6.   C. an she wen' up to da five feet

7.   C. I couldn' swim 'cause I could only go I could only go up to da three feet not to da five

8.   C. an' she started drowning

9.   C. dis is at schoo'

10. C. an' I went an I got 'er

11. C. but I couldn' I couldn' hold 'er dat long

12. C. den, I jus' told 'er hold on ta my shoulders

13. C. an' I started swimmin' back

14. C. and at da sea, I mean it's like a river, when my sister started drownin'

15. C. an she wen' way way in da back

16. C. an' she it woulda been it came up to here

17. C. den I wen't it came up ta here ta me

18. C. I wen' an' got 'er picked her up like dis dis when I's about eight

19. C. I could pick my sister up if I put her I on my shoulder

20. C. I put her on swimming'

21. C. started walkin' back da shore

22. C. told 'er to sit dere for moment

23. C. she calmed down

Rasheed has two events thematically linked to each other. In line 1 the investigator introduces the topic for discussion. In line 2, Rasheed begins the narrative by introducing the main character (sister) in the narrative. In line 3, the adult asks for clarification of the first statement. It appears the adult has cut off the narrator in line 2 because the statement ends with "an." In lines 2, 4, 6, and 7 the narrator uses repetition ("da five feet") to emphasize the danger of swimming in the deep end of the pool. In line 4, the audience is told that the narrator's sister did not know how to swim. In line 5, he repeats that his sister did not know how to swim. In line 6 there is a repetition of the beginning of the statement in line 4. Lines 5 and 6 are a repetition of line 4. Lines 7 and 8 serve as the complicating action of the narrative: The sister started drowning (line 8). In line 7, the narrator builds up suspense by emphasizing that he could not swim. In line 9, the narrator adds more detail to the setting. In lines 10 through 13, the narrator resolves the complicating action by rescuing his sister. In lines 14 through 23, the narrator tells about another event of hero behavior.

In this event the setting is at the sea. The same main character went too far into the water ("way way"). In lines 16 and 17 the narrator uses hand gestures to indicate how deep the water was in comparison to his and his sister's heights. Lines 18, 19, and 20 are similar to lines 12 and 13. The narrator repeats the same resolution from the first event. It is not clearly stated that the sister is drowning, but the event is implied in line 18. Lines 22 and 23 end the narrative by describing the reaction of the main character to the narrative.

To summarize, this narrative has two events that are thematically linked together by the topic of being a hero. The narrator uses repetition throughout the narrative to emphasize points. Both events move from a beginning to a complicating action, and then on to a result.

The next narrative is by Shaka, a 10-year-old African American male. The prompt was: "When I was younger, my brother and I were down South visiting my aunt. My brother climbed a tree in the backyard and fell out of the tree onto a wagon. He hurt his leg and had to go to the hospital to get stitches."

1.	A. Have you ever had to get stitches?
2.	C. no, but my little brother
3.	C. he um, he was real young
4.	C. I think he was two years old
5.	C. an' my mother was drivin'
6.	C. an' my my uncle was in fron' seat
7.	C. an' me an' my younger cousin dat lives in Baltimore,
8.	C. she's eight years old
9.	C. her name is Whitney
10.	C. an' my little brother was sittin' next to us
11.	C. an' we was lookin' aroun'

12.   C. an' he started playin' with da door

13.   C. an' the door was unlocked

14.   C. an' he opened the door an' he fell out the car

15.   C. an' he was he was flippin' back

16.   C. an' he his head was busted open an' he had da get stitches

17.   C. an' me an my cousin Whitney was sittin' in the back o' the car cryin'

18.   C. because he fell out the car

19.   C. my mother kep' goin'

20.   C. an he did then my uncle Al said, "Rhonda stop the car because he fell out the car"

21.   C. an' she got out the car

22.   C. and, she was actin' crazy

23.   C. an' she got'im

24.   C. an' we took 'im to the hospital

25.   A. what do you mean she was actin' crazy?

26.   C. like she like OH MY GOD she like MY BABY

27.   A. so you took him to the hospital and what happened?

28.   C. and he got a cast around his head

29.   C. an' den, he got stitches an' we brought him home

In line 1 a question is on the floor. The narrator answers the question in line 2 and introduces the main character. In lines 3 and 4 the narrator piles on more details about the main character. In line 5, we have the setting of the narrative and the introduction of another character. Lines 6, 7, 8, and 9 introduce three more characters (uncle, narrator and cousin).

In lines 10-14 the complicating action is presented. In lines 11 and 12 the narrator adds detail to the narrative: all of the children were in the back seat. The two older children were looking around while the younger child was playing with the door. In line 13 the narrator adds the detail that the door was unlocked. In line 14, the younger child falls out of the car.

In line 15 the narrator uses figurative language ("was flippin back"). The visual image of a child falling and flipping is bought to mind. In line 16 the narrator gives the resolution and answers the question about someone having to get stitches. In lines 17 through 29, the narrator uses performative techniques to enhance the telling of the event.

The narrator uses the evaluative word "cryin" to assess the situation with the little brother. In line 20, the narrator uses dialogue to describe the adults' actions in the narrative. The uncle notices that the child has fallen out of the car. In line 22, the narrator describes the mother's reaction of her child falling out of the car. In line 26, Shaka uses a different voice (mother) in the statements: "Oh my God" and "My Baby." Shaka ends the narrative by repeating the resolution started in line 16 ("he had da get stitches"). In addition, the narrator informs the audience that the child was brought home from the hospital.

To summarize, this narrative was coded as performative. Shaka narrates a story about his younger brother who has fallen out of the car. As a result of the fall, the child had to go to the hospital and received stitches for a wound to the head. Shaka used evaluative language, dialogue, figurative language, and different perspectives throughout the narrative. These strategies emphasize the performative aspects of the narrative.

The next narrative produced by Tia, an 8-year-old African American female, was coded as reactive following the episodic framework.

Tia

1.	A. Can you tell me a time when you were scared?
2.	C. O.K. (sucks teeth) I was sleepin' right.
3.	A. un huh
4.	C. I wasn' sleepin
5.	C. My de door was shut
6.	C. Everythin' was shut acc
7.	C. I was in my room acc
8.	A. un huh
9.	C. I think somebody couldn't set the fire
10.	C. They set the house on fire
11.	A. un huh
12.	C. I think so when I am sleeping (pause) an' I hate fires
13.	A. un huh
14.	C. Cause when you are sleepin' you can't smell smoke
15.	C. An' when I'm sleepin' I have asthma
16.	A. un huh

17. C. an I might start coughing

18. C. an I don't know if there is a fire stress

19. C. is gonna be a fire stress

20. A. un huh

21. C. cause the people upstairs in my house dey do drugs

22. A. un huh

23. C. an they sell like at 12 o'clock at nigh' or one o'clock or two o'clock in the morning pitch, intonation

24. A. un huh

25. C. an' I don' know if dey do drugs but they do do drugs

26. A. un huh

27. C. because they be smokin' at night

28. C. I can tell, um upstairs um

29. C. cause dere's a hole in our room

30. A. un huh

31. C. and you can smell de smoke come down

32. A. un huh

33. C. but dey do do drugs

34. A. un huh

35. C. but sometime it close de hole close up

36. A. un huh

37. C. cause we be puttin like

38. C. we be knocking' wood on de

39. C. we be puttin' wood on dea

40. A. un huh

41. C. an we only ting we been puttin' wood down dea

42. A. Oh OK

43. A: So tha's why you were scared?

44. C. un huh

45. A. cause you don't want there to be a fire

46. C.un huh because I have asthma

In line 1 of the narrative, the researcher elicits the narrative using a question prompt. The narrator begins in line 2 about a past event of sleeping. Line 4 is opposite of line 2 for the event of sleeping. In line 2, she is sleeping, while in line 4, she is not sleeping. In lines 5, 6, and 7 the narrator describes the setting of the event. In lines 5 and 6, the narrator repeats "was shut" two times. Also, in lines 6 and 7 the narrator accelerates her rate of speech. In the lines 9, 10, 12, 14, and 15, Tia uses the strategy of repetition for emphasis. In lines 18 and 19, the narrator stresses "is" and "be" for emphasis. In lines 21 and 25, the phrase "dey do drugs" is repeated. In lines 25 and 33, the phrase "dey do do drugs" is also repeated. In lines 27, 37, 38 and 39, Tia uses the habitual "be" to describe actions by herself and family members that occur frequently. Tia ends the narrative by telling the listener why she was concerned about smoke and fire "because I have asthma."

Tia interacts with the audience throughout the narrative. There are 17 interactions between the narrator and the listener. Tia moves back and forth in time, which is similar to Terri's performative narrative. Tia does not talk about one concrete episode, but ponders the possibility of a particular situation. Within this narrative, the possibility of having asthma is always imminent. At first she implies that having an asthma attack is out of her hands, but by the end of the narrative, the narrator has solved the problem by closing the hole in the ceiling.

Tia's narrative is very complicated and multi-layered. The narrator is planning throughout the production of the narrative. By the end of the narrative, she moves from a position of powerlessness to a position of being empowered. The narrator understands some of the perils of drug abuse such as people trafficking late at night, the possibility of a fire, and the possibility of a health risk due to smoke inhalation.

Eight narratives were coded as being "performative." In this structure the segments were tied together with an overall theme. Each segment is a 'scene' in the narrative. Within each segment, paralinguistic cues are used to link together a segment. The performative narratives tend to be long and include interaction between the narrator and the audience. Within this structure, the primary goal of the narrative is a performance.

The performative nature of narratives produced in the West African and African American cultures has been discussed by researchers previously (e.g., Okpewho, 1992; Smitherman, 1977). There are numerous occasions in which the performative narrative is commonly produced within the African American community, such as is seen in the African American church. On Sunday mornings across the country, many African Americans gather to hear the storyteller (minister). How well his/her message is received depends on the "performance" he/she produces. For example, the narrative Terri produced might have links to African American discourse style she experiences in her church. Terri called upon the cultural knowledge of her audience regarding Rosalind, which is also

done in the African American church by the preacher. The following excerpt is
from Terri's narrative:

44   C. but now shes grown .. shes fast .. !and shes fresh

45   C. she cuss ..^ she wear lipstick

46   C. she smokes cigarettes

47   C. tha:s bad

Stylistic features enhance a narrative when evoking cultural images. The con-
notations of the words *grown, fast* and *fresh* are all related in this context. First,
they are terms that you would hear used by people with a southern background to
describe a young person who is out of control. "Grown" (in isolation) refers to a
young person who is acting beyond his/her age or inappropriately to the culture's
norms and expectations. In this case, "grown" is produced with other descriptors
and the meaning is related to a young person's sexuality. The term "fast" is similar
to "grown" (again referring to the Rosalind's sexual behavior), while "fresh" indicates that Rosalind is attracting older boys to her. By using these descriptors, Terri
indicates Rosalind's innocence as a child is gone. The narrator describes in lines
45 and 46 the results of being "grown." Rosalind is using profanity, wearing lipstick
and smoking cigarettes. These are behaviors that a young person may use to act
beyond her age of innocence. In short, the narrator is conjuring up an image of a
teenager whose behavior is unacceptable to what she's been taught by socialization in the African American community. The narrator is assuming that the listener shares the same values, or least understands them. The evaluative language
used by the narrator is usually used by people generations above her age. In order
for the narrator to use this sort of language and to understand its meaning at 8
years old, she has to have heard evaluative language in her environment. This narrative also indicated her ability as storyteller to inform the listener with cultural
icons that are familiar to both the narrator and to her audience.

The second goal of imparting information is similar to the "moral centered" narrative. Community and relationships are also highlighted in the "performative"
narrative. However, the "performative" narrative differs in how the information is
presented. In this narrative, the narrator participates differently in the narrative
process than in the "moral centered" narrative. In the "performative" narrative,
community members are in the center of the narrative, while the narrator is on
the outskirts using herself as a vehicle to keep the narrative moving.

Another similarity between the "performative" narrative and the "moral centered" narrative is the concept of time. In the "performative" structure, there is a
circular time pattern present in the narrative. In Terri's performative narrative,
the narrative begins in the present (line 1); it then goes to cover events in the past

(lines 3 - 8); it returns to the present (lines 9-26); it goes back to the past (lines 27-43); it returns to the present (lines 44-47); it shifts to the future (48-52); it returns back to the present (lines 53-58); it goes on to the future (lines 59-64); it returns back to the present (lines 66-69); finally, it ends in the future (lines 70-77). The narrator moves from the present to either the past or the future with fluidity. The audience is left with the task of understanding why each element of time is important in the narrative. Observing time as a multidimensional concept helps the audience understand that the present, past and future are interconnected to each other.

Smitherman (1977) has asserted that narratives that involve departures from the theme to make one's point utilize Black rhetorical strategy. Similarly, Okpewho (1992) has defined digression as a departure from the main theme of a narrative to address an object or person at the storytelling event, or to comment on an issue which is related in some way to the theme of the narrative. These strategies are seen in the following excerpt from a talk by Bernice Johnson Reagon during the 1989 National Black Child Institute National Conference:

1. There's a man in Southwest Georgia.

2. named deacon Freddie Smith

3. When ever he opens a service

4   he says halalu, halalu, halalu halalu, halalu my Lord

5. I'm going to see my friends oh yeah halalu

6. Now he's been a member of Mt. Antioch church

7. and has not missed a Sunday since he joined in 1928.

8. He opens most of the services

9. and he opens with that song

10. When you think of concerts that wouldn't fit

11. but when you think of songs preparing the air in which you have to

12. have to exist

13. you understand that you get up in the morning

14. and and you go to the bathroom

15. you get up in the morning

16. you eat breakfast you brush your teeth

17. there are just certain things you do

18. so that you 'll be all right

19.   The same man talked about letting go.

20.   He talked about in terms of doing hymns

21.   and seeing younger generations choose not to do that same style.

22.   and understanding that he could speak about the beauty of them

23.   and how important they were

24.   but also understand that he could not make anybody do it.

25.   But he could locate what he was going to go out doing

26.   that his job was not to make sure the younger generation carried

27.   this repertoire

28.   his job was to be with them as much as he could

29.   and always when they heard him

30.   they would hear the repertoire and

31.   he had choice but anytime he could be with them

32.   he would be with them

33.   and he carried his sound with him

34.   and there is no child who's come through that church

35.   whether they ever song that song or one of his hymns

36.   who would not be able to sing halelu, halelu, halelu

37.   and it works interesting because I grew up in a house

38.   my mother put onions in everything

39.   I couldn't stand onions

40.   and I was picking the onions off my plate

41.   and putting them to the side.

42.   I put onions in every thing I cook

43.   you can't make people do,

44.   you have to let people go

45.   and when you let them go you have to locate

46.   it doesn't mean you're not going to still be a force in their lives

In this excerpt from a larger text, there are two digressions from the narrative to make points related to the theme. The narrator begins with a story about a deacon in Georgia with the theme of choices and not forcing people to do what you do (lines 19 and 24). In lines 13 to 17, the narrator digresses from the narrative to emphasize the point of existing in this environment. In lines 37 to 42 , there is a second departure from the story of the deacon to a short narrative about making choices. In line 43, the narrator returns to her point of the story by stating "you can't make people do, you have to let people go."

Moreover, narratives can also be viewed as a type of discourse that reflects the talk of one's culture. This view represents narratives in a broader sense than the evaluative or episodic schemas. By viewing narratives as a social process one can examine how narrators not only tell about the past but also how they negotiate around the present and possible future events. Again, by examining the contexts in which narrators tell particular narratives to particular listeners, one must take a different position than simply an a priori hierarchical category (as they are reflected in the Labovian and episodic models). Some of the narratives that were labeled performative by the author were coded as "reactive" and "leapfrogging" according to episodic and evaluative analyses, respectively. (These two structures are on the lower end of the hierarchical category.) These patterns have been described as a series of statements that may or may not be causally related to each other. Peterson and McCabe (1983) reported that these patterns were found most often with 4-year-olds.

This description is a narrow view of narrative analysis and may not adequately describe narratives. Narrators employ different structures which give shape to experiences in their world. These experiences may not fit into a neat linear pattern but are shaped as they are constructed by both the narrator and the listener. These narratives are complex; I found that a thematic analysis of them yielded a fuller description than the findings that could have been made had they been coded as being reactive and/or as using the leapfrogging structure.

PART III
Research to Practice

The purpose of Part III is to provide implications for educating African American students in schools in the United States. The research presented in this book examines narratives produced by African American children. The research was grounded in West African and African American storytelling traditions. The narratives were analyzed using traditional and nontraditional approaches. The results across all analyses indicate that African American children in this study produced a repertoire of narrative structures. Some of the narrative structures were linear school like- structures, while others appear to have links to West African and African American storytelling structures.

Chapter 8 outlines educational implications for working with African American students with the perspective that narratives are grounded in the social and cultural practices of the African American community. In this chapter, I discuss educational implications under four broad categories: home-school mismatch; teacher expectations; culturally relevant pedagogy and, finally, examples of narrative instruction.

8
Implications for Educating
African American Students

And of the cultural forms that emerged from their complicated historical process, only black music-making was as important to the culture of African-Americans as has been the fine art of storytelling. Telling ourselves our own stories-interpreting the nature of our world to ourselves, asking and answering epistemological and ontological questions in our own voices and on our own terms-has as much as any single factor been responsible for the survival of African-Americans and their culture. The stories that we tell ourselves and our children function to order our world, serving to create both a foundation upon which each of us constructs our sense of reality and a filter through which we process each event that confronts us every day. The values that we cherish and wish to preserve, the behavior that we wish to censure, the fears and dread that we can barely confess in ordinary language, the aspirations and goals that we most dearly prize-all of these things are encoded in the stories that each culture invents and preserves for the next generation, stories that, in effect, we live by and *through*. (Gates, 1989, p. 17)

Gates, description of the purposes of storytelling in the African American community has been used as a framework for the research presented in this book. In this book, I have discussed the origin of the African American narrative tradition in order to establish its historical and societal context, reviewed the literature on narrative structures among African and African American cultures, given procedures, and presented finding on episodic, evaluative, performative and moral centered analyses of narratives.

Findings of the study

The results reported in this book reveal that when examining the narrative structures of African American children, a priori taxonomies such as episodic and evaluative analyses can be applied. These taxonomies may reflect universal language principles that African American children utilize when producing narratives. Indeed, there is literature (Rumelhart, 1975; Stein & Glenn, 1979) suggesting the existence of a universal story schema across cultures and languages. At the same time, however, other literature (Heath, 1983; Michaels, 1981) points to differences in narrative production by different cultural groups. Because research on narrative production by culturally and linguistically diverse groups, as well as what constitutes universal principles in narrative production, is limited, these issues require further study.

The results indicate that using a thematic analysis may reveal information not found within traditional analyses. The thematic analysis within this study suggested that African American children's narratives could be classified as "classic," "moral centered," and "performative." These structures were not found with evaluative and episodic analyses. When analyzing narratives from diverse linguistic groups, educators may find that a thematic analysis is useful for describing narrative production.

The results also suggest that African American children produce and use sophisticated language. For example, the evaluative and episodic findings in this study were more sophisticated than those reported in Peterson and McCabe's (1983) corpus. Children in this study produced 66% of their narratives in the classic pattern, as is described through evaluative analysis. In comparison, the children in Peterson and McCabe's (1983) corpus produced 51% of their narratives in the classic pattern. In addition, the children in this study produced 74% of their narratives as either complete or complex as classified by story grammar analysis. In Peterson and McCabe's corpus, 55% of the narratives produced were coded as complete or complex. The results suggest that children in this study produced complex narratives with higher frequency. This finding conflicts with the long-standing, prevalent contention in education that African American children's language production is deficient. The results of this study contradict the deficit language model proposed by earlier studies during the 1960s and 1970s.

Relevance and Educational Implications

In this section I discuss educational implications of understanding narrative productions among African American children using three broad categories: home-school mismatch; teacher expectations and culturally relevant pedagogy; and examples of narrative instruction.

Home-School Mismatch

Children are socialized into literacy through the activities and experiences in their everyday lives with peers and adults regarding how to think about, talk about, and use literacy before they enter school (Heath, 1983). Scott and Marcus (2001) suggest that all children come to school with certain literacy experiences that have materialized from their daily experiences in their homes and communities.

Even with current information on home literacy practices, not all of the experiences into which the children have been socialized are valued or utilized by the school systems (Scott & Marcus, 2001). McCarthy (1997) found that teachers had more information about middle-class students than about working-class students from diverse cultural and linguistic backgrounds, resulting in a literacy curriculum more closely tied to the home practices of middle-class families. Consequently, mismatches between home and school literacy practices are evident, and may be one cause of the perceived low school literacy skills of some African American children.

Michaels (1981) has suggested that oral narration prepares children for reading and writing. Children move from oral language during the preschool years to reading and writing in the elementary years. There is a concern that many African American children are lagging behind European American children (Snow, Burns, & Griffin, 1998) in academic abilities, most specifically reading achievement. In 1996 the underachievement of African American children in education was in the spotlight because of the Ebonics resolution by the Oakland, California school board, requiring all schools in the district to participate in the Standard English Proficiency (SEP) program. Oakland's school board proposed the SEP educational program for teachers, which would focus on features of AAE so teachers would be able to help children move from home to school language in an effort to improve academic achievement. It is important to note that there are educational programs where African American children are achieving. Delpit (1995) notes that at the Nairobi Day School in East Palo, California, African American children scored three grade levels above the national average. This is just one example of an educational institution where achievement is expected by the teachers. Researchers (Irvine, 1989; King, 1991) have suggested that high teacher expectations and culturally appropriate pedagogy help African American children do better academically. In the following paragraphs I examine the importance of teacher expectations and the use of culturally appropriate pedagogy with African American children.

Teacher expectations

Rosenthal and Jacobson's (1968) research indicates that students' performance is linked to teachers' expectations. It is important for teachers of African American children to have the same standards as for middle-class European American children. Winfield (1986) uses four categories of teachers in urban schools: tutors, general contractors, custodians, and/or referral agents. Tutors are defined as teachers who expect children to achieve and know that the children's achievement is their responsibility. General contractors believe children can achieve with the help of teacher resources outside the classroom. The teacher with the custodian mindset does not believe the children can achieve but maintains the level in which the children are currently achieving. Finally, referral agents try to refer as many children as possible into special education. Teacher expectations can make learning experiences for children positive and motivational. In addition, it is important for the children to see themselves in the curriculum.

Culturally Relevant Pedagogy

In a recent lecture to educators Asa Hilliard (2001) emphasized things "we know we know." The first on his list was that "all children can learn." "We know as educators and speech language pathologists that all children are capable of learning and achieving academic success." Researchers have indicated in recent years that all children may not learn the same way using multiple approaches that incorporate different learning styles. Rickford (1999) studied narratives and reading comprehension of African American junior high school students, interviewing the teacher of the classroom. The teacher had this to say about learning in his classroom:

We need to adjust to a lot of different learning skills, to the different learning styles of children. I believe that everybody in my classroom can learn. And I believe that if we learn the different learning styles, we can address those so the we can meet the needs of our children. (Rickford, 1999, p.50)

Some researchers (Rickford, 1999; Ladson-Billings, 1994 ; Smitherman, 1999) have suggested that by using a culturally relevant pedagogy would help bridge the gap between home and school cultures. In addition, it provides a way for students to maintain their cultural integrity while succeeding academically (Ladson-Billings, 1994). Specifically Ladson-Billings (1994) has defined this pedagogy as:

> Culturally-relevant teaching is a pedagogy that empowers students
> intellectually, socially, emotionally, and politically by using cultural
> referents to impart knowledge, skills, and attitudes. These cultural
> referents are not merely vehicles for bridging or explaining the
> dominant culture; they are aspects of the curriculum in their own
> right. (pp. 17-18)

Ladson-Billings (1994) studied eight African American classrooms where children were performing at or above grade level in a district where African American children on the whole were performing below grade level. In the classrooms where the children were successful, the teachers practiced three overall concepts: conception of self and others; social relationships in the classroom; and knowledge of self.

In the first concept, conception of self and others, the first belief that was that all children can learn. In these classrooms children were not labeled "at risk" because they were African American children. Second, the teachers also focused on the process of teaching and were not fixed on one notion of teaching. Third, the teachers were invested in the community in which they taught. They either lived in the community or bought goods and services in the community. Fourth, the teachers saw teaching as a way of giving back to the community. The last belief in the concept of self and others was that children came to school with a knowledge and it was the teacher's goal to pull the knowledge out of the student.

The second concept Ladson-Billings (1994) discusses is social relationships. In this concept the relationships between the students and teacher are seen as flexible. In some of the classrooms the students taught the lessons while the teachers sat and listened. Teachers tried to connect with all students by looking for knowledge or expertise that might be unique to that particular student. In the classrooms studied, teachers focused on the whole class for academic success rather than on individuals. This fostered collaborative efforts by students and limited competitiveness.

The third concept was knowledge of self. Teachers and students constructed and shared knowledge. Teachers examined the curriculum critically and helped students engage in a variety of forms of critical analysis. For example, students critiqued social studies textbooks that might be used in the district. Finally, teachers used a variety of ways to assess students' progress in school, such as tests and portfilios.

In the next section I present three examples of researchers and teachers using culturally relevant pedagogy to expand African American narrative production in classroom settings. In all three examples literature from African American culture is used as a framework for instruction.

Examples of Narrative Instruction

In a storytelling project with 4 -year-old African American children in an urban preschool, my colleagues and I attempted to use a culturally relevant teaching project for oral and written narrative development. This storytelling project was organized in a manner that would elicit children's narratives in both spoken and written contexts. Twice a week, a member of the research team would begin by telling or reading a story to the students who were gathered on a rug area. The stories were deliberately varied in mode (told and read) and genre (e.g., folktales, modern children's stories, personal stories). All stories were either traditional African American (e.g., folktales) or books about African American life by African or African American authors, or personal stories about events in the lives of the African American members of the research team.

An excerpt of a storytelling session (Bloome, Champion, & Katz, 1997) is presented. In this session a member of the research team read the story <u>Catskinella</u> by Virginia Hamilton (1985) to the children and then asked for volunteers to tell a story.

1   T: O.K. Jimmy

2   Nice and loud Tommy so Ms. (name of teacher in the back) can her you

3   O.K. everybody quiet

4   J: This a story about the three little pigs.

5   The first little pig

6   T: Shhhhh

7   J: The first little pig says his house out of 'traw

8   it was out of 'traw and the wolf came and said knock, knock let me in.

9   The frighten pig cried no, no, no not by hair of my chinny, chin, chin

10   and it huff and puff and blow the house down

11   and den he went to the second little pig house

12   and the second little pig's house was made out of

13   (Unidentifiable student - Sx): straw

14   J: sticks

15   Sx: straw

16   J: sticks

17   Sx: straw

18   T: O.K. this is Jimmy's story O.K.

19   Sx: (indecipherable comment)

20   J: It wasn't very strong

21   T: It might change a little

22   J: and the wolf came and said knock, knock let me in

23   and it said no, no, no not by the hair of my chinny, chin, chin

24   and he huff and puff and blow the house down

25   and he

26   and the wolf run all the way to the third little pig's house

27   and the third little pig made his house out of bricks

28   It was very strong and the wolf came and said knock, knock
        let me in

29   and the frighten pigs cried no, no, no

30   not by the hair of my chinna, chin, chin

31   den I huff and puff and blow your house down

32   den den he didn't blow the house down

33   (Students): (clapping starts)

34   J: that's the end

35   T: Awl right

36   Sx: Can I read one

37   Very good version of three little pigs

On lines 13 to 17 there is a brief argument about whether the house was made out of straw or sticks, until the teacher stepped in and stated that it was Jimmy's story and that he could change the story if he wanted. Notice that the children's right to transform stories was reinforced at the end by the teacher in line 37. (As an aside, line 36 is an interesting comment by a child who is bidding for a chance to tell a story; the students have not yet gone to their tables for storywriting. It may be that the child views the storytelling as similar to what the teacher did or has generalized reading to include storytelling or has confused the storytelling at that time with the storytelling they do after their storywriting, which is occasionally described as reading their stories from their author books).

There would be about 6 or 7 children (20 children in the class) who told stories for about 10 minutes. After the oral storytelling by the children, the researcher would then ask the children to think of a story to write in their author books (a hand made book with blank construction paper stapled together. They went to their desks and wrote a story in their author books.

Members of the research team and the teachers walked around to each child and requested that the child tell them the story that was being written. The researchers and teachers wrote down verbatim what the children said. The children were allowed about 20 minutes of this activity. The final activity of the storytelling session involved volunteer children reading their stories from the author books for the last 15 minutes of the session.

The finding of the project suggests that children take up the narrative styles, structures, and content that are made available to them, and then "experiment" with those styles, structures, and content. The sources available for students to take up various narrative styles, structures, and content include formal instruction (e.g., teachers reading traditional stories, peers, families, television), informal instructional contexts (e.g., talking with the teacher or peers during an instructional activity), family contexts, and others. The range of available sources provides the possibilities out of which a repertoire of narrative styles, structures, and content can be developed.

Another example of narrative instruction that uses culturally relevant pedagogy is a study by Rickford (1999). In this study, Rickford (1999) used African American literature texts from two genres- folktales and contemporary narratives to teach reading and narrative comprehension. There were a total of six texts used: The Woman and the Tree Children (an African Masai tale), Brer Rabbit Falls in Love (an African American tale), Why Apes Look Like People (an African American tale), The Runaway Cow (contemporary), Remembering Last Summer (contemporary), and Ride the Red Cycle (contemporary).

To assess comprehension of narrative texts, Rickford asked questions in four areas: General Questions (2), Literal Meaning Questions (3), Interpretive Reading and Critical Evaluation Questions (3), and Creative Reading Questions (2). There were a total of 11 questions. One question from each of the categories is presented:

General Questions (2)

On a scale of 1 to 6, rate how much you like this story. Circle the answer that most shows the way you feel. This question was ranked on a Likert Scale ranging from 1 to 6.

Literal Meaning Questions (3)

Why did the old woman think she had live an unhappy life?

BEST WORST POSSIBLE

 A Because she had grown old

 B Because she had no husband and children

 C Because she had a husband but no children

 D Because she had no friends

 E Because she was wicked, Old woman

Interpretive Reading and Critical Evaluation Questions (3)

Moral Judgment Question

Was it right or wrong for the woman to lose her temper and scream at the children?

Right _____ Wrong _____

Give a reason for your answer. It was right, OR It was wrong, because
. . .

Creative Reading Question (1)

Problem Solving Question

How would you treat your tree children if you were the old woman in the story? Write about what you would say to them or do with them after they broke your special dish? (pp. 99 -113)

Rickford's (1999) results indicated that the narrative choices motivated African American middle school students to become more engaged in reading and narrative comprehension.

Lee (1993) investigated the use of signifying as a scaffold teaching strategy to interpret complex implied relationships in African American fiction in secondary classrooms with African American students. For the purpose of the research, Lee (1993) developed an instructional unit for students. The instructional unit was designed with four phases.

Phase One. In the first phase students examine data sets. Teachers provide students with samples of signifying dialogues. These dialogues serve for examination by the students. The students respond to the following questions: (1) Does each speaker mean exactly and literally what each says? (2) How do you know? (3) What does each speaker actually mean? (4) How do you know?

Second Phase. Expand students' metalinguistic knowledge about signifying and its properties. Students read two expository articles, one about signifying, "Signifying, Loud Talkin and Marking by Mitchell- Kernan (1981) and Nobody Mean More Than to me Then you and the Future Life of Willie Jordan(1988).

Third Phase. In the third phase students work in small groups to write their own signifying dialogues.

Fourth Phase. In the fourth phase students apply the strategies they learned in the first phase of the unit to the short story "My Man Bovanne" by Toni Cade Bambara and the first chapter of "Their Eyes Were Watching God " by Zora Neal Hurston. Finally, students read and interpreted two novels.

Lee's (1993) results indicate that the instructional model enabled students to interpret figuratively dense works of African American fiction. I have presented three examples of teachers using culturally relevant teaching to enable African American children to achieve using the cultural wealth that they bring to schools.

Directions for Future Research

In the previous analyses and discussions, I have examined narrative production with African American children aged 6 to 10 years. The participants in this study produced personal narratives (accounts). Future research should focus on exploring the production and development of different narrative types by African American children, as described by Heath (1986): recount, accounts, eventcasts, and stories (fiction). Currently, there is a paucity of information on narrative types by African American children. Research in this area will inform researchers and educators on the developmental aspects of narrative types.

Another area of research where little information exists is narrative production and its relation to literacy development in African American children. Only a few researchers (Lee, 1993; Rickford,1999) have examined this area. This type of research can be valuable for teachers when developing literacy curriculum for children.

Conclusion

This study has focus on the production of narratives by African American children. The research design was drawn from an ethnographic perspective. African American children were selected from a low- income community in the Northeast, where children participated in two after- school programs located a mile apart. Video-taped and audio-taped data was collected on site at the after-school programs. A total of 15 children who met criteria for participation in the narrative activity were video-taped and audio taped as they told personal stories to a familiar adult. All videotapes were transcribed for each child. A total of 71 narratives were subjected to analysis. Narratives were analyzed using different procedures: thematic analysis, evaluative analysis, episodic analysis, and a micro-sociolinguistic analysis. Results indicate that some African American children produce complex narratives using a priori taxonomies. In addition, the results indicate that some narratives when analyzed qualitatively, may have connections to the African American community.

In conclusion, it is important for educators to realize that storytelling is a very important function in life for all cultures. The way in which a story is structured may be influenced by the children's socialization process. Therefore, children tell stories that are appreciated in their communities. These stories, when brought to school, must be valued and appreciated for their complexity and creativity.

Appendix A

Narratives by Participants

Below is a narrative sample produced by each participant.

Participant: Caren

>Eight -year-old female
>
>### PROMPT: STITCHES / HOSPITAL

Adult: Have you ever had to go to the hospital?

Adult: Oh, what happened?

Child: I have asthma an I have wards [warts]

Adult: So when was the last time you went to the doctors

Child: Las year, an' I'm goin' to da dentis' on nex' Friday.

Adult: So what happened when you went to the doctor last year?

Child: I' was jus' 'bout my warts.

Adult: So what happened when you went in?

Child: They had put cold, I mean dry ice on it.

Child: an' they had burned in

Child: I peeled it off

Child: an' they got bigger an' bigger

Child: an' I have more growin' in

Child: an tha's all

Participant: Dora

>Nine -year-old female
>
>### PROMPT: STITCHES / HOSPITAL

Adult: Do you know anybody who had to get stitches?

Child: mm, a boy in my secon' grade class name Evan he he was running

Child: an' da lady tol' him not be runnin'

Child: an' he kep' on runnin'

Child: He didn' listen to her

Child: an' he fell straight on da footsteps where you step at

Child: an' it's like a curve thing

Child: an' dere was ice on it

Child: an' he fell

Child: an' an' den da nex' day he didn' come to school

Child: so so when he didn' come to school he had ta um he had da get stitches

Child: an' den a few weeks later he came in

Child: an' he got da stitches

Child: an' it's was nasty

Child: dey was nasty

Child: dey were black

Participant: Fatima

Ten -year-old female

PROMPT: SCARED

Adult: Can you tell me a time when you were really really scared?

Child: when when when it's dark in my room on Halloween 'cause my my

Child: my cousin he he cut all da lights off

Child: I wasn' asleep

Child: but my cousin he cut all da lights off

Child: an' I started to scream

Child: an' my cousin he kep' laughin'

Child: an' my mother she tol' my cousin's mother

Child: an' my cousin got in trouble

Child: an' den another time when we went trick or treatin' on Halloween night

Child: an' den my cousin he had he was like a um one o' my cousins was a

Child: an' my other cousin he was um Freddy Kruger an he had dees claws

Child: an' I was scared 'cause he was I was scared

Child: an' las' night I had dream dat me me an you know Tierra? Me an' Tierra

Child: me an' Tierra was playin' outside in da dark in da middle o'da night

Child: an' an' Freddy Kruger came and kep' chasin us

Child: an' all my cousin we kep' runnin' da store

Child: I had a dream 'bout dat

Participant: Jason

Seven-year-old male

PROMPT: GRANDMA / TROUBLE

Adult: Oh you know

Child: mm-mmm. . . 'cause, um when we go outside an den when we go far den she gets

Adult: so where are supposed to stay?

Child: in 'a backyard but we went to go jump off a roof

Adult: You went to jump off a roof? What happened?

Child: nothin'

Adult: Did you jump off the roof?

Child: yeah!

Adult: Well something happened then! Tell me what happened

Child: we went um we went to the behind the store

Child: there was just a little roof an den da roof was up to the ceiling

Child: an' then there was a big snowbank almost actually it was right like

Child: an' den we jumped down

Child: dat's all we did

Child: that's that's why my mom got mad at us

Participant: Lakesha

Seven-year-old female

PROMPT: STITCHES / HOSPITAL

Adult: he had to be taken to the hospital

Child: das what happened to my big brother

Child: he got pushed in the glass

Child: he had to git twenty-five stitches in his butt

Adult: Really? And then what happened?

Child: den he felt better

Child: 'cause he didn't, 'cause everytime he used to take a bath the stitches

Child: an now he only got three stitches more

Child: an its goin go away too

Participant: Lola

Ten-year-old female

PROMPT: GRANDMA / TROUBLE

Adult: Can you tell me about a time when you got in trouble?

Child: Well, one time one day I was playin' an' my brother my brother kept

Child: When I was making clothes for my dolls when I play with them

Child: an' I was making clothes for for my friends

Child: an' I made a pillow making my las' pillow, then my pillow fill wit'

Child: an' he came

Child: an' he kept knocking on the door

Child: everytime he knock on da door, I poke myself wit the with the needle

Child: an' my all my clothes would start, my walls would start to shake because

Child: then when I got up, I tol' I started yellin at him that I was gonna, you

Child: an' I was gon' hit 'im

Child: but my mom said, my mom started yellin' at me

Child: she said if you hitcha' brother ya gonna be in your room for the rest

Child: take control o' yourself in your room until you learn how to start to

Child: 'cause I wasn't brought dat way an' you weren' brought dat way

Adult: and so what happened?

Child: she tol' my brother to get outta my room

Child: an' he couldn' come back in there

Adult: Wow

Child: and y mom said it wasn' my fault

Child: she said she'd be angry at him too

Child: sometime everytime she cookin dinner an all he always say, What's

Child: what're we havin'

Child: an' she kep' sayin wait an' see, wait an' see

Child: always be some kind o' surprises

Participant: Malik

Ten-year-old male

PROMPT: MISCELLANEOUS

Adult: So what happened?

Child: when um, because when because we can't hang on da hoops up upstairs

Child: an' den an' den an' den I had hung on da hoop

Child: an' den he, he said get off da hoop off da hoop

Child: an I be like, the hoop was up her fo' dat an hang on it

Child: an' an' um an' dunk an' shoot an' all that stuff

Adult: and then what happened?

Child: an' den, an' den he be like tellin' me get off, get off, get off

Child: an' den he like you suspended, you suspended

Adult: and so what were you suspended for?

Child: nothin' He he he jus' playin' wit' me.

Child: He wasn' playin' wit me like see like if if I got off

Child: an' den, he wouldn' say notin' no more

Adult: Oh so he was trying to make you get off?

Child: mm-hmm

Participant: Rasheed

>   Nine-year-old male

PROMPT: HERO

Adult: Can you tell me a time when you were a hero? Have you ever been a hero?

Child: yes my sister wen' up in da five feet an

Adult: Up in the what?

Child: in da five feet 'cause she couldn' swim

Child: an' I couldn' swim neither

Child: an she wen' up to da five feet

Child: I couldn' swim ' cause I could only go I could only go up to da three feet

Child: an' she started drowning

Child: dis is at schoo'

Child: an' I went an I got 'er

Child: but I couldn' I coudn' hold 'er dat long

Child: den, I jus' told 'er hold on ta my shoulders

Child: an' I started swimmin' back

Child: and at da sea, I mean it is like a river, when my sister started drowning

Child: an' she it woulda been it came up to here

Child: den I wen' it came up ta here ta me

Child: I wen' an got 'er picked her up like dis dis is when I's about eight

Child: I could pick my sister up if I put her I on my shoulder

Child: I put her on swimmin'

Child: started walkin' back to da shore

Child: told 'er to sit dere for moment

Child: she calmed down

Participant: Rashida

>   Nine-year- old female

PROMPT: SICK

Adult: Has there been a time when you've been sick?

Child: I was sick one time.

Child: I couldn' stop bein' sick

Child: I was like in kindergarten or preschool at da time

Child: I got so sick really sick like I couldn' stop coughin

Child: so so so I couldn' to ta school

Child: den from night till morning my dad stayed wit' us dat night

Child: den he came in our room an' he xx 'cause we never went to sleep

Child: an' den aan den' he came an' gave me some pineapple in da day

Child: an um den I was in my room 'cause we had carpet in my room green

Child: an' puked on it

Child: an' den I had ta hurry up an' run to da bafroom

Child: my room is right here an da bafroom is here

Child: an my mom's room is here

Child: so I kep' throwin up could' stop

Child: an' one time I was drinking milk

Child: a roach kep' crawlin' it was crawlin' up my leg roach was crawlin' up

Child: den I was drinkin' my milk

Child: and I was do milk was in my mouth

Child: I went "aaah" a roach

Child: an' da milk fell outta my mouth

Child: an' fell right on da roach

Child: an I was get off roach get off get off roach!

Participant: Shaka

Ten -year -old male

PROMPT: STITCHES/HOSPITAL

Adult: have you ever had to get stitches?

Child: no, but my little brother did

Child: he um, he was real young

Child: I think he was two years old

Child: an' my mother was drivin'

Child: an' my my uncle was in fron' seat

Child: an' me an' my younger cousin dat lives in Baltimore she's
    eight years

Child: her name is Whitney

Child: an' my little brother was sittin' next to us

Child: an' we was lookin' aroun'

Child: an' he started playin' wit' da door

Child: an' the door was unlocked

Child: an' he opened the door an' he fell out the car

Child: an' he was, he was flippin' back

Child: an' he, his head was busted open an' he had da get stitches

Child: an' me an my cousin Whitney was sittin' in the back o' the
    car cryin'

Child: my mother kep' goin'

Child: an' he did then my uncle Al said, Rhonda stop the car
    because he fell out

Child: an' she got out the car

Child: and, she was actin' crazy

Child: an' she got 'im

Child: an' we took 'im to the hospital

Adult: what do you mean she was acting crazy?

Child: Like she was like oh my Gosh she was like my baby

Adult: so you took him to the hospital and what happened?

Child: and, he got a cast around his head

Child: an' den, he got stitches an' we brought him home

Adult: that must have been a scary experience for you all

Child: an' he busted his lip in preschool

Adult: how did he bust his lip?

Child: no, no teacher was payin' attention to 'm

Child: an' no I think he was younger

Child: I think he was a toddler

Child: an' he fell out the chair an' busted his lip open an' he had
    to get stitches

Paricipant: Sharon

>Seven-year-old female

PROMPT: SICK

Adult: How about a time when you were sick?

Child: I we', I went to the doctors

Child: an' my mom, she had to see if I had asthma

Child: an' I had to go to the um store to get my medicine

Child: an' uh, they didn' have it

Child: an' I had to for 'em them to make it

Child: an um, my mom, she wen' back again

Child: an' so she kep' on goin' back an' back an finally it was done

Child: an I xx , when I got in the car an' she got it

Child: I had to drink some, I's nasty

Participant: Shateka

>Seven-year-old female

STITCHES/HOSPITAL

Adult: what happened to them? (sister and brother)

Child: we had a my mother ran dis, dis um dis dis dis stop sign

Child: an' dis truck was comin' an he hit da da da passenger side dat my mo

Child: an' it hit it an' my ear was bleedin' on dis side

Child: an' my brother was sittin' near da window

Child: an' my brother was sittin' near da window

Child: an' da window like like it da da one of da windows jus cracked open a

Adult: an' then what happened?

Child: an' every time my mother ca' after dat everytime my mother combed

Child: an' one time, another acciden' happen, like a couple o' days after dat

Adult: and what happened?

Child: I don' know 'cause my mother tol' me but she didn' tell me every thin'

Participant: Tia

Eight –year- old female

PROMPT: STITCHES/HOSPITAL

Adult: did you ever know somebody that had to go to the hospital?

Child: I know somebody dat hurt

Adult: somebody that what?

Child: I know somebody dat had to go da de hospital

Adult: Oh why did they have to go to the hospital? What happened to them?

Child: it was my grandmother

Adult: un hun

Child: she xx high heel on

Child: she had what

Child: she had high heels on

Child: it was at midnight

Child: all of us was there

Child: and plus me an' my sisters

Child: an my cousin an das it

Adult: un hun

Child: jus four of us

Child: not my brotha he was at home

Adult: ok so what happened?

Child: so my grandmotha was to go downstairs

Child: dea was no railage

Adult: oh was no railage

Child: firs' time she broke her lag, she was at her house

Child: da had some railage but it was ricketty

Child: den she carryin some suitcases

Child: an she fell and broke her leg

Child: but she didn' get no stitches

Adult: oh

Child: all she did is got crutches

Adult: oh

Participant: Terri

Eight –year- old female

PROMPT: GRANDMA/TROUBLE

Adult: Has that ever happened to you? When you make a mistake?

Child: yeah she always, my mom she always yell at me

Child: or my gran mother she she always say "you did that on purpose, I'm gonna . . ."

Child: den she start yellin' at me

Child: tell me to go to my room an' stuff

Child: when I do it, an accident

Child: then I say sorry

Child: then one time I had my mom she let me wear her necklace

Child: I didn' break it

Child: I put it up on my mom's TV an it wasn' broken

Child: an' my brothers, he was playin' Shandel he's four

Child: he was playin' wit it

Child: an I put it back on the TV

Child: I guess he picked it up an touched it an broke the necklace

Child: and I said I didn't break it though

Child: an, an I said I'm not lyin'

Child: al didn't break it

Child: Shandel was playin' with it

Child: an den she said well Shandel probably broke it

Child: but then, but she yellted at me

Child: so I wen' to my room an' clean my room up

Child: mommy I'm not lying

Child: I did'n' break it

Child: She said I can get out

Adult: She said what?

Child: she said I can get out my room

Child: ok

Participant: Tyrone

Six-year-old male

PROMPT: STITCHES/HOSPITAL

Adult: an he had to get stitches

Child: I got, gotta 'nother story

Child: um one time um I was in my room

Child: an' I playin' wit my frien's

Child: an den dey made all my mess, an' den, all da mess in my room

Child: den when dey was gone, my mom my mom tol' me to clean up all de m

Child: an' I didn' do it

Child: 'cause my frien's put all da mess up

Child: cause dey, an' den I said, when dey come back dey have ta clean it ba

Child: But I had to clean all my toys

Child: an my mom had to clean all da clothes

Appendix B
Linguistic Features of African American English

In the following paragraphs, I provide a description of African American English.

Linguistic Features of African American English

There are several phonological and grammatical features that are described as being characteristic of African American English. In the area of phonological variation, African American English differs from Standard American English in word, sound, and contrast variability. Some of the most common phonological features are discussed in the following paragraphs.

Phonological

Phonological Variation. In the area of phonological variation, one can see that African American English differs from Standard English in a number of ways such as word, sound, and contrast variability. Moreover, it has come to be recognized that African American English has systematic rules for consonant reduction and the use of final consonants.

Word Variability. Word variability is random pronunciation of words such as *skreet* for *street*, *thew* for *threw*, *ax* for *ask*, *bidness* for *business*, and *posed to* for *supposed to* (Labov & Cohen, n.d., *English in Black and White*). There are also a few words that stress the first syllable instead of the second as in Standard English usage. For example, *PO-lice* and *DE-troit* are words that use this stress pattern.

Sound Variability. The vowel sounds have noted variability between Black speakers and White speakers, according to Burling (1973). Blacks who were raised in the North preserved characteristics of the southern pronunciation /ai/ in words such as *time*, *my*, *find*, *ride*, etc. In African American English, vowel contrasts are lost under limited linguistic environments. These contrasts are not lost in Standard English. In addition, there are words that are homonyms in African American English. For example, *oil* becomes *all* and *during* becomes *doing*, to name a few (Dandy, 1991).

The Standard American English /th/ sound can be produced voiced or voiceless in the beginning position. In the production of the word this, the /th/ sound is voiced, while in the word think, the /th/ sound is voiceless. In African American English, in place of the voiced /th/ the /d/ sound is substituted so that this becomes dis; in the voiceless production thin becomes tin. In AAE, the middle and ending /th/ can be pronounced as /f/ or /v/. An example of /th/ substitution is baf for bath. Wiv for wife is an example of /v/ substitution of /th/.

In African American English, final consonants are variable in their pronunciation. (The consonants with variability in pronunciation will be discussed separately.) With African American English, in words that end in the /s/ consonant plus another consonant the last consonant is deleted. For example disk becomes dis and desk becomes dess. When these consonant cluster words are pluralized, /es/ is added instead of /s/, so dis becomes disses and des becomes desses.

In the production of the postvocalic /l/ and /r/ in African American English, deletion and substitution rules are applied. The postvocalic /l/ and /r/ may be weakened such as in the words *hep* for *help* and *ho's* for *horse*. There can also be deletion when /r/ or /l/ is followed by an /o/ or /u/ such as ca'ol for *carol*. In the words *sister* and *brother*, the final /r/ can be substituted as /uh/ so that sister becomes *sistah* and brother becomes *brothuh*. Also, in AAE the final /t/ and /d/ may be deleted or weakened. The /t/ may become a glottal stop, or it can be lost completely. The /d / may be changed to a /t/ or it can be eliminated. An example of when /d/ is deleted occurs in the statement *I burn myself* for *I burned myself*. In addition, the /t/ and /d/ may be lost in final consonant blends. In African American English, the sounds /g/, /d/ and/ b/ can be produced as /k/, /t/ and /p/, so that pig becomes *pik*, lid becomes *lit* and lab becomes *lap*.

Grammar

The Possessive. African American English speakers may omit possessive suffixes, or they may be used some of the time and omitted in other instances. When they are omitted, other ways of expressing possession are used. To express possession, the name of the possessor is put directly in front of the name of the possessed without any explicit sign of possession at all. For example, *That man hat is on the table* is understood because of its context.

Plurals. Plurality operates in African American English very much as it does in Standard English, with a few exceptions. One exception is seen in the word *desk*, which is pronounced as *dess*, and becomes *desses* when pluralized. The same is true for *test* and *ghost*. Some irregular nouns undergo "double" pluralization such as in the words *mens, children,* and *foots* for *feet*. When Standard English nouns are classified by a plural quantifier, the /s / is often deleted. For example, *I have five cents* becomes *I have five cent*. In third- person singular present tense, the /s/ is deleted in structures, as is seen when *he runs* becomes *he run*.

Past Tense. The final /ed/ can be weakened or omitted in African American English in the past tense, the past participle, and in derived adjectives. Structures such as *they talked yesterday* becomes *they talk yesterday; he has finished the job* becomes *he has finish the job*; and *he is a brown-eyed baby* becomes *he is a brown-eye baby* (Wolfram & Fasold, 1974).

Multiple Negation. In African American English it is acceptable to have more than one negative in a sentence. The dialect accounts for this, as Smitherman (1977) stated, ". . . if the statement consists of only *one sentence*, negate every item; if the statement consists of two or more sentences combined as one, all negatives indicate "positives," and all negatives, *plus one positive* indicate "negatives" (p. 31). Examples of multiple negation are seen in the sentences *There ain't nobody ready yet* and *Ain't none them people worth nothing.*

Contracted /is/, /are/, /'ve/ and /'s/. Wherever is and are can be contracted in Standard English, they may be deleted in African American English (Wolfram & Fasold, 1974). As a result, *he's handsome* becomes *he handsome*, and *they're cute* becomes *they cute.* In African American English, the auxiliary forms of "to have" that are contracted in Standard American English are deleted in the present tense. Therefore *she's done well* becomes *she done well* and *they've gotten together* becomes *they gotten together* (Wolfram & Fasold, 1974).

Perfective "Done". Baugh (1983) gives the following guidelines for the use of perfective done: "Done is a perfective marker, and it is used with moderate regularity in colloquial contexts where suitable perfective comments are appropriate" (p. 75). Dillard's (1973) investigation of the origin of African American English states that one of the more interesting facts about done is its occurrence in other pidgin and Creole related languages. Examples of sentences using the perfective done that would be appropriate in African American English are: *I done my schoolwork*, and *I done did her hair* (Smitherman, 1977).

Stressed "Been". In the earlier studies of *been*, most scholars observed that perfective meanings were usually attached to the word; moreover, they were always found in contexts with progressive verbs (see Stewart, 1967; Fickett, 1970; Fasold & Wolfram, 1975; Dillard 1972; Baugh, 1983, p. 81). Rickford has observed that *been* can be used with stative verbs. Been can also be "used to show emphasis, regardless of the time that has elapsed since an action took place" (Smitherman, 1977, p. 23), as is seen in the sentences *We been lived here* and *She been told him she needed the money.* An example of stress on *been* to show emphasis as in *She been there*, uttered with stress on the *been*, means that the individual wants to emphasize the fact that the individual has been wherever she is for a long enough period of time that it's an established fact (Smitherman, 1977, p. 23).

Aspectual Marking with Steady. According to Baugh (1983), the use of the word *steady* can be used with progressive verbs in sentences like *Leon steady trippin* and *She steady be runnin her mouth* (p. 86).

Invariant "Be". Labov and Fasold have concluded that there are two functions associated with the invariant be: the habitual and the durative. An example of a durative function was given by Baugh (1980) in the sentence *And we be tired from the heat, but he just made everybody keep on working.* In this example, the activity extends over a period of time but it is not habitual. An example of habitual function can be seen in the sentence *he be sick*, meaning that he is sick all of the time, or that every time you see him, he is sick (p. 772).

Intonation and Prosody.

The use of prosody in African American English has been examined by a few researchers. Tarone. (1973) examined intonation contours with African American and European American adolescents. She found a wider pitch range that extended into higher pitch levels with the African American English speakers than with the Standard American English speakers. In addition, there were more level and rising final pitch contours on all sentence types for African American English speakers. Tarone also found that there was the use of falling pitch contours to ask yes/no questions in a formal situation. This finding correlates with that of Loman (1967), who had similar results. Within less formal situations, however, yes/no questions ended with level and rising final contours. Loman's results correlate with the findings of Green (1990), who examined ending intonation contours of yes/no questions from natural speech from speakers of Lake Arthur, Louisiana. In Green's study, children had ending contours that were either at a sustained high level or at an upstepped high level.

Michaels (1981) examined the intonation contours used by European American and African American first graders during the production of narratives spoken during "sharing time" in the classroom. Both groups produced different types of contours. The European American children used "vowel elongation and a gradual rising intonation contour stretching over the last word or two of a tone group" (Michaels, 1981, p. 426). These children used a final rising contour to indicate more information was coming and a final falling contour to indicate that narrative was completed.

The African American children also used vowel elongation, but they had a high-rise/mid-fall contour (level). Michaels (1981) further stated that Black children's prosody was characteristic of "sharp pitch modulation, giving the talk an almost singsong quality" (p. 426). Instead of using a final-falling intonation contour, African American children used a level final contour. This contour indicated that more information was to come.

Michaels and Collins (1984) examined prosody within narrative production of two groups of children: one European American, and the other African American. In the topic-centered narratives produced by European American children, the intonation pattern consisted of a gradual "rising contour stretching over the last word or two of a tone group" (Michaels & Collins, 1984, p. 222). In this style of narration, children established a topic with a rise in tone, while a falling tone was used to end a topic. European American alternated between a rise and a fall in tones to elaborate on a topic. This finding was in contrast to the topic-associating style produced by African American children, who signaled a major shift in perspective with a pause followed by a sustained pitch on and. In this style of narration, children used vowel elongation instead of falling and rising tones to signal a change in topic.

Vocabulary.

In 1949, Lorenzo Turner scrutinized the question regarding the vocabulary of the Gullah dialect with his work titled, *Africanisms in the Gullah Dialect*. Turner found approximately 6,000 words of African origin during his 15-year study of Sea Island (an area in South Carolina and on the Georgia coast). Charleston, South Carolina, was used as a port of entry for slavery up until the middle of the 19th century where African Americans lived in isolation for centuries. This may account for the late survival of African vocabulary in that region (Dillard, 1972).

During the late 1960s, British linguist David Dalby examined the usage of Africanisms in Standard American English. He cited over 80 words that were borrowings from African languages. Dalby researched the meanings of selected words borrowed from Africa and found a connection between the West African linguistic reversal process of using negatives to refer to positive meanings and its usage in current African American English vocabulary.

Smitherman (1977) has compiled a list of four traditions from which Black semantics may be rooted: fine talk, coded dialect, music and *cooltalk*, and the Black church tradition. Fine talk is the use of exaggerated language to make a point. We see an example of fine talk from a 19-year -old black male when he states, "*Naw, it ain true. He being fictitious*" instead of "*He lying*" (p. 47). Coded dialect, defined as using language to hide the speaker's meaning from whites, is another tradition that has been used by African Americans. Music and cooltalk are traditions deeply rooted in the African American experience. Vocabulary has been developed from musical expressions from the Black folk tradition and from terms used by musicians themselves in their lyrics or in their general speech. Examples of music and cooltalk vocabulary are *gig* (reference to jazz musician's job), and *funky* (down to earth soulfully expressed sounds).

The Black church tradition of call response and the belief that the human soul can triumph over adversity have influenced African American English vocabulary. An example of vocabulary from this tradition is "gittin the spirit" which means to show deep emotion and express feeling of one's soul by body movements and gestures. The traditional Black church retained the African belief in spirit possession.

The vocabulary of African American English is important not only to the African American community, but it has also entered into mainstream society. Closely related to African American English vocabulary is its usage. This can be heard in the oral tradition of the African American community.

Bibliography

Ani, M. (1994). Yurugu: An African-centered critique of European cultural thought and behavior. Trenton: Africa World Press, Inc.

Asante, M. (1990). African elements in African-American English. In J. Holloway (Ed.), Africanisms in American culture (pp. 19-33). Bloomington: Indiana University Press.

Awona, S. (1965). La Guerre d'Akoma Mba contre Abo Mama. Abbia, 9 180-214.

Bailey, G. (1987). Are black & white vernaculars diverging? American Speech, 62(1), 32- 40.

Bailey, B. (1965). Toward a new perspective in Negro Englishdialectology. American Speech, 40(3), 171-177.

Bailey, G. & Maynor, N. (1985). The present tense be in southern black folk speech. American Speech, 60(3), 195-213.

Bambara, T. C. (1972). My man Bovanne. In T. C. Bambara (Ed.), Gorilla, my love (pp. 1-10). New York:Random House.

Baugh, J. (1984). Steady: Progressive aspect in black vernacular English. American Speech, 59(1), 3-12.

Baugh, J. (1983). A survey of Afro American English. Annual Review of Anthropology, 12, 235-54.

Baugh, J. (1983). Black street speech: Its history, structure, and survival. Austin: University of Texas Press.

Bauman, R. (1986). Story, performance, and event: Contextual studies of oral narrative. Cambridge, England: Cambridge University Press.

Beier, U., & Gbadamosi, B. (Eds.). (1959). Yoruba poetry. Ibadan: Government Printer.

Bloome, D. (1989). Classroom and literacy. Norwood, NJ: Ablex Publishing.

Bloome, D., Champion, T., & Katz, L. (1997). Preschoolers as storytellers and storymakers in an urban preschool, Invited Presentation, National Council of Teachers of English, Detroit, MI.

Bloome, D.; Champion, T.; Katz, L.; Mortin, M.; & Muldrow, R. (2001). Spoken and written narrative development: African-American preschoolers as storytellers and storymakers. In Kamhi, Pollack and Harris; (Eds.), Literacy in African

American Communities. (pp. 45-76). Mawah, New Jersey, Lawrence Erlbaum Associates, Inc.

Brewer, J. M. (1972). American Negro folklore. Chicago: Quadrangle Books.

Bruner, J. (1985). Narrative and paradigmatic modes of thought. In E. Eisner (Ed.), Learning and teaching: The ways of knowing (pp. 97-115). Chicago: University of Chicago Press.

Burling, R. (1973). English in black and white. New York: Holt, Rinehart, and Winston.

Champion, T. (1995) .A description of narrative development and production amongAfrican American English child speakers. Unpublished dissertation, University of Massachusetts, Amherst, MA.

Champion, T. (1999). Personal communication.

Champion, T. (1998). "Tell me somethin' good": A description of narrative structures among African American children. Linguistics and Education, 9(3), 251-286.

Champion, T., Katz, L., Muldrow, R.., & Dail, R. (1999). Storytelling and sto-rymaking in an urban preschool classroom: Building bridges from home to school culture. Topics in Language Disorders, 19(3): 52-67.

Champion, T., Seymour, H., & Camarata, S. (1995). Narrative discourse among African American children. Journal of Narrative Life History, 5(4), 333-352

Cole, L. (1980). A developmental analysis of social dialect features in the spon-taneous language of preschool black children. Unpublished doctoral dissertation, Northwestern University, Evanston, IL.

Cope, T. (1968). Izibongo: Zulu praise poems. Oxford: Clarendon Press.

Dalby, D. (1972). The African element in Black American English. In T. Kochman (Ed.), Rappin' and stylin' out communication in urban Black America (pp. 170-186). Urbana, IL: University of Illinois Press.

Dandy, E. (1991). Black communications: Breaking down the barriers. Chicago: African American Images.

Delpit, L. D. (1995). Other people's children: Cultural conflict in the classroom. New York: The New Press.

Deng, F. M. (1973). The Dinka and their songs. Oxford: Clarendon Press.

Dillard, J. L. (1972). Black English. New York: Vintage Books.

Dubois, W.E.B. (1961). The souls of black folks. Originally written 1903. Greenwich, CT.: Fawcett Publications Organization Ltd.

Dubois, W. E. B. (1939). Black folks, then and now. New York: Holt.

Fasold, R. & Wolfram, W. (1975). Some linguistic features of the Negro dialect. In P. Stoller (Ed.), Black American English (pp. 49-83). New York: Delta Publishing Co., Inc.

Fasold, R. (1969). Tense and the form "be" in Black English. Language, 45(4), 763-776.

Foster, Michele. (1982). Sharing time: A student run event. (ERIC Document Reproduction Service No. ED 234 906).

Foster, M. (1989). "It's cooking' now": A performance analysis of the speech events of a black teacher in an urban community college. Language in Society, 18(1), 1-29.

Foster, M. (1992). Sociolinguistics and the African American Community: Implications for literacy. Theory Into Practice, 31(4), 303-311.

Gates, H. (1989). Introduction: Narration and cultural memory in the African American tradition. In L. Goss & M. Barnes, (Eds.), Talk that talk: An anthology of African-American storytelling (pp. 15-19). New York: Simon & Schuster, Inc.

Gee, J. (1985). The narrativization of experience in the oral style. Journal of Education, 167(1), 9-35.

Glenn, C. G. & Stein, N. (1980). Syntactic structures and real world themes in stories generated by children. Technical Report. Urbana: University of Illinois, Center for the Study of Reading.

Goodenough, W. H. (1981). Culture, language, and society. Menlo Park: California: Cummings.

Goodwin, M. (1990). He-said-she-said talk as social organization among black Children. Bloomington: Indiana University Press.

Gomez, M. (1999). Exchanging our country marks: The transformation of African identities in the colonial and antebellum south. Chapel Hill: The university of North Carolina Press.

Goss, L. & Barnes, M. (1989). Talk that talk: An anthology of African-American storytelling (pp. 15-19). New York: Simon & Schuster, Inc.

Green, L. (1990). Intonational patterns of questions in Black English: Some observations. Unpublished manuscript.

Gumperz, J. (1982). Discourse strategies. Cambridge, England: Cambridge University Press.

Hall, R. (1990). African religious retentions in Florida. In J. Holloway (Ed.), Africanisms in American culture (pp. 98-118). Bloomington: Indiana University Press.

Hamilton, V. (1985). The People could fly. New York: Alfred A. Knopf

Heath, S. B. (1983). Ways with words: Language, life and work in communities and classrooms. Cambridge, England: Cambridge University Press.

Heath, S. B. (1986). Taking a cross-cultural look at narratives. Topics in Language Disorders, 7(1), 84-94.

Herkovitz, M. J. (1941). The myth of the Negro past. Boston: Beacon Press.

Hester, E. (1996). Narratives of young African American children. In. A. Kamhi, K.

Pollock, & J. Harris (Eds.), Communication development and disorders in African American children: Research, assessment, and intervention (pp.227-246). Baltimore, MD: Paul H. Brookes Publishing.

Hicks, D. & Kanevsky, R. (1992). Ninja turtles and other superheroes: A case study of one literacy learner. Linguistics and Education, 4(1), 59-105.

Hicks, D. (1988). The development of genre skills: A linguistic analysis of primary school children's stories, reports, and eventcasts. Unpublished doctoral dissertation, Harvard University.

Hurston, Z.N. (1990). Their eyes were watching God. New York: Harper & Row.

Innes, G. (1974). Sunjata: Three Mandika Versions. London: School of Oriental and African Studies.

Hyon, S. & Sulzby, E. (1994). African American kindergarteners' spoken narratives Topic associating and topic centered styles. Linguistics and Education, 6(2), 121- 152.

Irvine, J. (1989). Cultural Responsiveness in Teacher Education: Strategies to Prepare

Majority Teachers for Successful instruction to minority students. Paper presented at the annual meeting of Project 30, Monterey, California.

Johnson Reagon, B. (1989). The Geraldine L. Wilson Seminar. Seminar presented at the National Black Child Development Institute Nineteenth Annual conference, Washington Hilton Hotel, Washington, D.C.

Jordan, J. (1988). Nobody mean more to me than you and the future of Willie Jordan. Harvard Educational Review, 58 (3), 363 - 74.

Kernan, K. T. (1977). Semantic and expressive elaboration in children's narratives. In S. Ervin-Tripp & C. Mitchell-Kernan (Eds.), Child discourse (pp. 91-102). New York: Academic Press.

King, J. (1991). Unfinished Business: Black student alienation and Black teachers' emancipatory pedagogy. In Foster, M. (ed.). Readings in equal education. New York: AMS Press.

Kochman, T. (Ed.). (1972). Rappin' and stylin' out: Communication in urban Black America. Urbana, IL: University of Illinois Press.

Kovak, C. (1980). Children's acquisition of variable features. Unpublished doctoral dissertation, Georgetown University, Washington, DC.

Labov, W. (1987). Are black & white vernaculars diverging? American Speech, 62 (1), 5-12.

Labov, W. (1975). The logic of nonstandard English. In P. Stoller (Ed.), Black American English (pp. 89-131). New York: Dell Publishing Co., Inc.

Labov, W. (1969). Contraction, deletion, and inherent variability of the English copula. Language, 45(4), 715-762.

Labov, W. (1972). Language in the inner city. Philadelphia, PA: University of Pennsylvania Press.

Labov, W. & Waletzky, J. (1967). Narrative analysis: Oral versions of personal experience. In J. Helm (Ed.), Essays on the verbal and visual arts (pp. 12-44). Seattle: University of Washington Press.

Ladson-Billings (1994). The DreamKeepers: Successful teachers of African American children. San Francisco: Jossey-Bass Publishers.

Lahey, M. (1988). Language disorders and language development. New York: Macmillan Publishing Co.

Lasebikan, E.L. 1955. Tone in Yoruba Poetry. Odu, 2: 35-36.

Lee (1993). Signifying as a scaffold for literacy interpretation: The pedagogical implications of an African American discourse genre. Urbana, Il: National Council of Teachers of English.

Levine, L. (1977). Black culture and black consciousness: Afro-American folk thought from slavery to freedom. New York: Oxford Univerty Press.

Liles, B. (1993). Narrative discourse in children with language disorders and children with normal language: A critical review of the literature. Journal of Speech and Hearing Research, 36(5), 868-882.

Liles, B. (1987). Episode organization and cohesive conjunctives in narratives of Children with and without language disorders. Journal of Speech and Hearing Research, 30(2), 185-197.

Liles, B. (1985). Narrative ability in normal and language disordered children. Journal of Speech and Hearing Research, 28(1), 123-133.

Loman, B. (1967). Conversations in a Negro-American dialect. Washington DC: Center for Applied Linguistics. (ERIC Document Reproduction Service No. ED 013455)

McCabe, A. & Peterson, C. (1985). A naturalistic study of the production of causal connectives by children. Child Language, 12(1), 145-159.

McCarthy, S.J. (1997). Connecting home and school literacy practices in classroomswith diverse populations. Journal of Literacy Research, 29, 145-182.

Michaels, S. (1981). "Sharing time": Children's narrative styles and differential access to literacy. Language in Society, 10(3), 423-442.

Michaels, S. & Collins, J. (1984). Oral discourse styles: Classroom interaction and acquisition of literacy. In D. Tannen (Ed.), Coherence in spoken and written discourse (pp. 219-244). Norwood, NJ: Ablex.

Michaels, S. & Cook-Gumperz, J. (1979). A study of sharing time with first-grade students: Discourse narratives in the classroom. In C. Chiarello, (Ed.), Proceedings of the Fifth Annual Meetings of the Berkeley Linguistics Society (pp. 647-660). Berkeley: Berkeley Linguistic Society.

Michaels, S. & Foster, M. (1985) Peer Peer Learning: Evidence from a student run sharing time. In A. Jaggar & M. T. Smith-Burke (Eds.), Observing the Language Learner, (pp. 143-158). Newark, DE: International Reading Association.

Mitchell-Kernan, C. (1981). Signifying, Loud and Marking. In A. Dundes (Ed.,). Mother wit from the laughing barrel (310-28). Englewood Cliffs, NJ: Prentice Hall.

Okpewho, I. (1992). African oral literature: Backgrounds, character, and continuity. Bloomington and Indianapolis: Indiana University Press.

Peterson, C. & McCabe, A. (1983). Developmental psycholinguistics: Three ways of looking at a child's narrative. New York: Plenum.

Pierrehumbert, J. (1980). The phonology and phonetics of English intonation. Unpublished doctoral dissertation. Massachusetts Institute of Technology, Cambridge, Massachusetts.

Polanyi, L. (1985). Telling the American story: A structural and cultural analysis of conversational storytelling. Norwood, NJ: Ablex.

Puckett, N. (1936). Folk-beliefs of the southern Negro. Chapel Hill

Reveron, W. (1978). The acquisition of four Black English morphological rules by black children. Unpublished doctoral dissertation, Ohio State University, Columbus.

Rickford, A. (1999). I can fly: Teaching narratives and reading comprehension to AfricanAmerican and other ethnic minority students. New York, NY: University Press of America.

Robinson, B. (1990). Africanisms and the study of folklore. In J. Holloway (Ed.), Africanisms in American culture (pp. 211-224). Bloomington: Indiana University Press.

Rosenthal, R. & Jacobson, L. (1968). Pygmalion in the classroom: Teacher expectations and pupils' intellectual development. New York: Holt.

Rumelhart, D. E. (1975). Notes on a schema for stories. In D. G. Bobrow and A. Collins (Eds.), Representation and understanding: Studies in cognitive science. (pp. 211-236). New York: Academic Press.

Scheub, H. (1975). The Xhosa Ntsomi. Oxford: Clarendon Press.

Scott, C. M. (1988). A perspective on the evaluation of school children's narratives. Language, Speech, and Hearing Services in Schools, 19(1), 67-82.

Scott, J.C. & Marcus, C.D. (2001). Emergent literacy: Home-school connections. In J. L. Harris, A.G. Kamhi, & K. E. Pollack (Eds.), Literacy in African American communities (pp. 77-98). Mahwah, NJ: Lawrence Erlbaum.

Seymour, H., Champion, T., & Jackson, J. (1995). The language of African-American learners: Effective assessment and instructional programming for special needs children. In B. A. Ford, F. E. Obiakor, and J. M. Patton (Eds.), Education of African-American exceptional learners: New perspectives. Austin: Pro-Ed.

Seymour, H. & Ralabate, P. (1985). The acquisition of a phonologic feature of Black English. Journal of Communication Disorders, 18(2), 139-148.

Seymour, H. & Seymour, C. (1981). Black English and Standard American English contrasts in consonantal development of four and five-year old children. Journal of Speech-Hearing Disorders, 46(3), 274-280.

Shuman, A. (1986). Storytelling rights: The uses of oral and written texts by urban adolescents. Cambridge, England: Cambridge University Press.

Smitherman, G. (1977). Talkin' and testfyin: The language of black America. Boston, MA: Houghton, Mifflin & Co.

Smitherman, G. (1999). Talkin that talk: Language, culture and education in African America. New York, NY: Routledge

Snow, C.E., Burns, M.S., & Griffin, P. (Eds.) (1998). Preventing reading failure in young children. Washington, DC: National Academy Press.

Spradley, J. P. (1979). The ethnographic interview. New York: Holt, Rinehart, and Winston.

Spradley, J. P. (1980). Participant observation. New York: Holt, Rinehart, and Winston.

Steffensen, M. (1974). The acquisition of Black English. Unpublished doctoral dissertation, University of Illinois: Urbana-Champaign.

Stein, N. L. & Glenn, C. (1979). An analysis of story comprehension in elementary school children. In R. Freedle (Ed.), New Directions in Discourse Processing (pp. 53-120). Norwood, NJ: Ablex.

Stewart, W. (1967). Sociolinguistic factors in the history of American negro dialects. The Florida FL Reporter, 6(2), 11, 22, 24, 26.

Stewart, W. (1968). Continuity and Change in American Negro Dialects. The Florida FL Reporter, 6(1), 34, 14-16, 18.

Stokes, N. (1976). A cross-sectional study of the acquisition of negation structures in black children. Unpublished doctoral dissertation, Georgetown University, Washington, DC.

Street, B. (1995). Social literacies. New York: Longman Publishing.

Tannen, D. (1989). Talking voices: Repetition, dialogue, and imagery in conversational discourse. New York: Cambridge University Press.

Tarone, E. (1973). Aspects of intonation in Black English. American Speech, 48(1), 29-36.

Taylor, O. (1988). Storytelling and classroom discrimination. Unpublished manuscript, Howard University, Washington, DC.

Traugott, E. (1976). Pidgins, creoles and the origins of vernacular Black English. In D. S. Harrison & Turner, L. (1949). Africanisms in the gullah dialect. New York: Arno Press.

Turner, L. (1949). Africanisms in the gullah dialect. New York: Arno Press.

Vaughn-Cooke, F. (1987). Are black & white vernaculars diverging? American Speech, 62(1), 5-12.

Vaughn-Cooke, F. (1976). The implementation of a phonological change: The case of resyllabification in Black English. Unpublished doctoral dissertation, Georgetown University, Washington, DC.

Westby, C. E. (1984). Development of narrative language abilities. In G. P. Wallach & K. Butler (Eds.), Language disabilities in school-age children (pp. 86-121). Baltimore: Williams and Wilkins.

Whitten, N. & Szwed, H. (1970). Afro-American anthropology: Contemporary perspectives. New York: Free Press

Williams, D. (1997). Black-Eyed peas for the soul: Tales to strengthen the AfricanAmerican spirit and encourage the heart. New York: Fireside.

Winfield, L. (1986) Teacher beliefs toward at-risk students in inner urban schools. The urban review, 1986, 18 (4), 253-267.

Wolfram, W. (1974). The relationship of White Southern speech to vernacular Black English. Language, 50(3), 498-527.

Wolfram, W. (1971). Black-white speech relationships revisited. In W. Wolfram & N. Clarke (Eds.), Black-white speech realtionships (pp. 139-161). Washington, DC: Center for Applied Linguistics.

Wolfram, W., & Fasold, R.W. (1974). The study of social dialects. Englewood Cliffs, NJ: Prentice-Hall.

Woodson, C.G. (1933). The miseducation of the Negro. Washington, D.C.: Associated Press.

Woodson, C. G. (1968). The African background outlined. New York: New University Press.

Wyatt, T. (1991). Linguistic constraints on copula usage in Black English child speech. Unpublished dissertation, University of Massachusetts, Amherst, MA.

Wyatt, T. & Seymour, H. (1988). The pragmatics of code-switching in Black English speakers. Paper presented at the Convention of the American Speech-Language-Hearing Association, Boston, MA.

Young, V. H. (1970). Family and childhood in a southern Negro Community. American Anthropologist, 72(2), 269-88.

Wyatt, T. (1991). Linguistic constraints on copula usage in Black English child speech. Unpublished dissertation, University of Massachusetts, Amherst, MA.

Wyatt, T. & Seymour, H. (1988). The pragmatics of code-switching in Black English speakers. Paper presented at the Convention of the American Speech-Language-Hearing Association, Boston, MA.

Young, V. H. (1970). Family and childhood in a southern Negro Community. American Anthropologist, 72(2), 269-88.

Zaharlick, A. & Green, J. L. (1991). Ethnographic research. In J. Flood, J. Jensen, D. Lapp, and J. Squire, (Eds.), The handbook of research in teaching the english language arts (pp. 120-175). New York: MacMillian.

Author Index

Subject Index